Heinemann **Scottish** History

THE Kingdom OF Scotland
IN THE Middle Ages

0-1450

...ong

Series editor: Jim McGonigle

Heinemann

Heinemann Educational Publishers
Halley Court, Jordan Hill, Oxford, OX2 8EJ
a division of Reed Educational & Professional Publishing Ltd
Heinemann is a registered trademark of Reed Educational & Professional Publishing Ltd

OXFORD MELBOURNE AUCKLAND
JOHANNESBURG BLANTYRE GABORONE
IBADAN PORTSMOUTH NH (USA) CHICAGO

First published 2002

ISBN 0 435 32094 7
04 03 02
10 9 8 7 6 5 4 3 2 1

Designed and typeset by Ken Vail Graphic Design, Cambridge

Illustrated by Steve Smith

Original Illustrations © Heinemann Educational Publishers 2002

Printed and bound in the United Kingdom by Bath Colourbooks

Picture research by Virginia Stroud-Lewis

Photographic acknowledgements

The author and publisher would like to thank the following for permission to
reproduce photographs:

Ancient Art & Architecture Collection/L. Ellison: 11B; Ancient Art & Architecture
Collection/R. Sheridan: 15F, 42B; Corbis/Arte & Immagini: 29D;
Corbis/Ludovic Maisant: 9D (right); Crown Copyright: 14D, 23B, 25C, 51B;
© His grace the Duke of Buccleuch: 60J; National Gallery Collection: 29C; National Library of
Scotland: 16A, 17B, 21B, 61A; National Museums of Scotland Picture Library: 5A, 7B, 8C,
15E; Scotland in Focus/D. Houghton: 26A; Scotland in Focus/G. Davis: 9D (left), 55G;
Scotland in Focus/M. Moar: 18D; Scotland in Focus/R. Weir: 7A; Scotland in Focus/S. Taylor:
46H; Scottish National Portrait Gallery: 46G; 50A; Skyscan: 22A; Stirling District Council/The
National Trust of Scotland: 58H; The British Library: 43D
Cover photograph © Smith Art Gallery and Museum

Written sources acknowledgements
The author and publishers gratefully acknowledge the following publications
from which written sources in the book are drawn. In some sources the wording
or sentence has been simplified.
R. Dargie, *Scotland in the Middle Ages 400–1450* (Pulse Publications, 1995): 12C
A. Duncan, *The Age of Ale and Brede* in *The Story of Scotland* (Sunday Mail, 1988): 37C
A. Erskine and A. Davidson, *Scotland at Peace, at War, 1263–1329* (Edward Arnold, 1978): 49I
M. Lynch, *Scotland: A New History* (Century, 1991): 18C

Contents

You will have already done some work on the Egyptians or the Romans, or perhaps the Greeks. These are ancient civilisations. Ancient history, or the classical period, is usually agreed to have finished around AD 410, when the Roman Empire ended. The next 1000 years of European history is the Middle Ages, and ends round about AD 1450.

Most historians agree that a number of important changes were starting to happen in Europe by this time, marking the beginning of modern times. These include the Renaissance, the invention of the printing press, and the beginning of European voyages of discovery. Thinking about the past like this, we can understand why the years from 400 to 1450 are called the Middle Ages, or the medieval period.

Questions

1. Make a timeline to show the last 2000 years. You can do this by copying the diagram shown below into your workbook.

| 1 AD | 400 AD | 1450 AD | 2000 AD |

▲ *A timeline for Scotland.*

2. Use a coloured pencil for this. On your timeline, carefully shade the area between AD 400 and AD 1450. Write the words 'Middle Ages' either on the area you have shaded or just above or below it.

3. Add some key events on to your timeline, starting with the end of the Roman Empire in AD 410. You can add others as you continue reading this book.

4. Explain in your own words what the phrase 'Middle Ages' means.

Scotland in AD 400

If we could be transported back in time to Scotland in AD 400, we would find that things were very different.

The landscape would look unfamiliar. There were no towns or cities. Nearly everybody lived in the countryside and worked on the land. There were no roads or bridges, only a few rough tracks. Much of the low-lying land was marshy, especially near rivers and streams, and the higher ground was usually moorland or forest. In the north and west of the country, the land was mountainous. Today, Scotland's population is about 5 million, but in AD 400 it was less than 400,000.

Most settlements were close to places which could provide people with safety against possible attacks, such as Trapain Law in East Lothian. People lived near the coasts and in river valleys to be near water and food supplies. Large areas of the country were uninhabited, but animals such as deer, wild boar and wolves were common.

Who are the Scots?

In the centuries after AD 400, several different groups of people settled in Scotland. They all played their part in helping to shape the identity of modern Scotland. The modern phrase 'multicultural society' means that we now live in a country containing people of several different ethnic groups and religions. This is not anything new. People from Ireland, Italy, eastern Europe, China, the Indian sub-continent and other places have come to live in Scotland over the past 150 years. They came to Scotland for many different reasons, but they and their descendants are now part of the Scottish nation.

In the same way, different people came to Scotland during the period 400–1450. They created a society that in some ways was as diverse as Scotland today. However, it took a long time before the ordinary people of Scotland began to think of themselves as one nation. This will be something you will learn more about in this book. The people of Scotland lived in tribes ruled by a chief. They were often at war with each other. The most powerful of these people were the Picts.

The Picts

We know very little about the Picts. In 400 they ruled most of the area north of the rivers Forth and Clyde, but were probably divided into tribes with separate kings. We do not know anything about their language, although their alphabet has survived. Most of our evidence is from archaeology; the Picts made beautiful stone carvings, which can tell us a lot about their way of life.

The Scots

From around 500, a tribe from Ireland crossed the sea to modern-day Argyll and began to settle in the area. They set up a kingdom called **Dalriata**. They were Gaelic speakers and their enemies called them 'Scots', which means raiders.

Source A

5

A Pictish sculptured slab, showing a horseman drinking. ▶

The Britons

The Britons lived in south-west Scotland, around the valley of the River Clyde. Their kingdom was called Strathclyde and their most important stronghold was the great fortress at Dumbarton. They spoke a Celtic language very like modern Welsh.

The Angles

The Angles had originally come across the North Sea from present day Germany or Denmark. They moved north to Lothian from Northumbria, pushing out the Britons, and capturing the fortress at **Dun Eidyn** (Edinburgh). The Angles spoke a Germanic language – Angle-ish, the ancestor of the English we speak today.

The areas in Scotland inhabited by the Picts, the Scots, the Britons and the Angles from 400–600. ▶

Many struggles took place between these groups of people. The most important battle took place in 685 near Forfar in Angus, at Dunnichen or Nechtansmere. Here, the Pictish king Brudei defeated an invading Anglian army, killing the leader, Egfrith of Northumbria. Historians think this was a very important event because it made sure that Pictland survived and limited the power of the Angles to south-east Scotland.

Questions

1. One of the most important jobs of an historian is to be able to compare historical evidence with the present day. Write down as many differences as you can between Scotland in AD 400 and Scotland now. Use appropriate sub-headings to help you, for example:

   - Population
   - Where people lived
   - Transport and communications.

2. Describe where the Picts, the Scots and the Angles lived in Scotland.

3. Why did people live close to hill forts, such as Trapain Law?

6

2 The coming of Christianity

We know very little about the religion of the early people of Scotland. However, it is clear that in the years after 400 they gradually became followers of the Christian religion. They were converted to Christianity by missionaries who came from Ireland and Northumbria.

One such missionary was Ninian. Very little is known about him, except that he was a Briton. Many believe that Ninian and his followers built a small stone church at Whithorn in Galloway, but historians and archaeologists are not sure. There may already have been a Christian centre in Galloway before Ninian arrived. What is certain is that most of the people living south of the River Clyde had become Christians by the end of the sixth century.

St Columba

The most famous of the early Scottish saints was Columba. From his base at the monastery on the island of Iona, he is supposed to have converted the northern Picts to Christianity. Much of our evidence about Columba comes from a book written about him 100 years after he died. The author was Adamnan, the abbot of the monastery at Iona. Adamnan tells us that Columba was a very holy man who could work miracles and foretell the future.

Source A

The abbey on the island of Iona. ▲

Source B

Modern historians tell a different story about Columba. They think he was an Irish prince who may have been sent to Dalriata (Argyll) for causing trouble at home. Once in Dalriata, he became an adviser to Aedan, the King of Scots, helping him to drive off attacks by the Picts, Angles and Britons. Together, Aedan and Columba did promote Christianity, but it was probably under Adamnan about a century later that the northern Picts became Christian (around 700–750). Columba, Aedan and Scottish kings after him for hundreds of years were buried on Iona, which even today is still a holy island.

◀ *The Brecbennach of St Columba.*

After Columba's death, some of his bones were put in a small box. This house-shaped shrine, the Brecbennach of St Columba, became the holiest of all objects in Scotland. Also called the Monymusk **reliquary** (a container for religious relics), it was carried into battle by the kings of Dalriata and later by the kings of a united Scotland as they thought it would offer them protection. In 1314, the Brecbennach was with Robert Bruce's army at Bannock Burn.

Questions

1. What information do we have about Christian missionaries in the sixth century?

2. What beliefs do people have about them?

3. **a.** Who was the most famous of the early Scottish saints?
   b. Where was he based?
   c. Why do you think Adamnan's evidence may not be trusted fully?

4. Explain why the Brecbennach of St Columba (Source B) is important in Scottish history.

St Andrew – Scotland's patron saint

Most people are familiar with the cross of St Andrew, which is the basis of the Scottish flag. But the story of St Andrew and how he became Scotland's patron saint is not so well known. Andrew was one of the disciples of Jesus, and it is said that he was crucified on an X-shaped cross known as a **saltire**.

The legend of St Regulus tells us that he was a priest from fourth century Greece who had to flee from his home. He escaped by ship, taking the remains of St Andrew with him. Eventually he landed on the Fife coast, building a church where the relics of St Andrew were kept. Another legend states that an eighth century king of Scots, Angus II, dreamt that he saw a saltire cross above his army the night before an important battle against the Angles. The next day, the Scots won the battle, and from then on the Scots army always carried the flag of St Andrew.

Modern historians believe that the cult of St Andrew developed because the shrine of St Columba in Iona was in danger due to attacks by Viking raiders in the early ninth century. Scottish kings were happy to use the legend of St Andrew as it made Scotland seem an important part of the Christian world.

Source C

A wooden staue of St Andrew – notice the saltire on his left arm. ▶

The Celtic and Roman Churches

By around AD 600, most people in Scotland, as in the rest of western Europe, had become Christian. However, there were disagreements about how this new religion should be organised. The Celtic Church, based in Ireland and Northumbria, was different in some ways from the Roman Church which most of the rest of Europe followed. The key argument was about how to calculate the date of Easter Sunday, the most important date in the Christian calendar, marking the resurrection of Jesus. In 664, Oswiu, a powerful king of Northumbria, decided to follow the Roman date for Easter. A **synod** (meeting) of important Church people was held at Whitby Abbey, where the Roman rules were agreed. Over the next 50 years, the distinct practices of the Celtic Church faded away.

Source D

A Celtic cross (left) and a Roman cross (right).

The following are the original differences between the Celtic and Roman Churches; by the seventh century the two were already coming together.

- Roman monks lived together in a monastery; Celts lived alone in bee-hive cells.

- Monks and priests shaved the top of their heads (called a **tonsure**) to show to everyone that they were Christians. Roman monks had a closed (or circular) tonsure; while the Celts had an open tonsure, in a wedge shape.

- Bishops were the most important people in the Roman Church and were appointed by the Pope (the head of the Church). Abbots, who were in charge of monasteries, were more important in the Celtic Church, and were chosen by the monks.

- Churches were the most important buildings in the Roman Church; whereas the Celtic Church preferred monasteries.

Questions

1. Who was St Andrew?

2. Why do historians think that St Andrew became so important?

3. What was decided at the synod of Whitby?

4. Explain in your own words at least three differences between the Celtic and Roman Churches.

9

Towards the end of the eighth century, Viking raiders from Scandinavia began to attack the coasts of Britain. Large number of these raiders settled in parts of Britain, including Scotland. We can include the Vikings (or Norse) as part of what has made Scotland the country it is today.

The Viking homelands

The present day countries of Denmark, Norway and Sweden were the homelands of the Vikings. It was difficult for the people there to make a living by farming, as much of the land was mountainous or had poor soil for growing crops. The Viking people were good sailors. Norway has many long, deep sea inlets, called fiords, often protected from the storms of the Atlantic Ocean by rocky islands. The calm waters of these fiords made it easy to learn to sail.

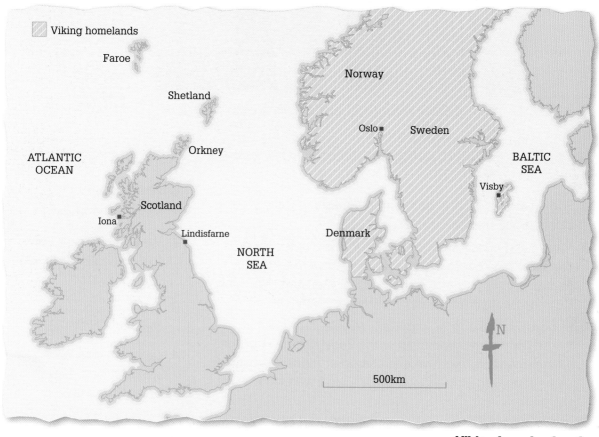

Viking homelands. ▲

There was a lot of quarrelling over scarce land and fishing rights, so it is not surprising that many Vikings took to the sea to earn their living. Some went to trade, others to raid, and others still to explore new places. Eventually some of the Vikings settled in lands they had explored. As you can see from the map, Scotland is close to the Viking homelands and so felt the full impact of these people.

The Vikings were able to go on long voyages because they developed ocean-going ships called **longships**. Several examples of Viking longships have been discovered by archaeologists. One of the best examples is the Gokstad ship, which was found near Oslo in Norway.

Source B

A Viking longship. ▲

The Gokstad ship was about 23·5 metres long (about the length of a tennis court) and 5·3 metres wide. It had sixteen pairs of oars, which were between 5 and 6 metres long. The oars were pushed through holes at the side of the ship. The mast was about 12·3 metres high, and had a square sail. There was a crew of about 60 men. In ships like these, the Vikings sailed across the Atlantic Ocean, almost certainly reaching North America.

Viking raids on Scotland

As we have seen from the map, Scotland lies close to the Viking lands. The first evidence we have of the Vikings coming to Scotland is in 795, when they attacked the monastery at Iona. At this time, the Vikings were not Christians, but they knew about the wealth which had been built up in the great religious centres such as Iona and Lindisfarne off the coast of Northumbria. Eventually, everything of value on Iona, including the relics of St Columba, was moved away for safety.

Source C

They returned in 802 and 806, killing 68 monks during their third raid on the island. In the year 825 they demanded that the monks hand over the sacred relics of St Columba which were kept in the monastery. When the monk Blathmac refused to say where this holy treasure was hidden, the Vikings put him to the terrible death of blood-eagling. His chest was cut open, his ribs were torn apart and his lungs ripped out.

An extract from a modern history book written in 1995.

The Vikings also captured people and made them slaves or took them as hostages. Monks were very well-educated and often came from wealthy families who could afford to pay a large ransom to free a prisoner. The wealth of the monasteries was stolen and traded with other merchants. The Vikings also took away grain and livestock to feed themselves and their families back home.

It is important to remember, however, that most of our evidence about Viking raids comes from chronicles of the time, written by Christian monks. In the Middle Ages, monks and other religious people were often the most educated people and were the ones who could read and write. Many of these monks would have experienced Viking raids and would have disliked their pagan religion, with their many gods. This may have made them and their writings biased against the Vikings.

Questions

1. Look at Source A. How can you tell that the author did not like the Vikings?

2. Explain why the author of Source A did not like the Vikings.

3. Where were the Viking homelands?

4. Try to work out as many reasons as possible why so many Vikings became raiders.

5. Why did the Vikings attack Christian centres such as Iona?

6. Why should historians be careful when using written sources about the Vikings?

Viking settlers in Scotland

After around 800, Vikings began to settle in Orkney and Shetland. Soon they were also settling in Caithness and northern Pictland (which they called Sutherland) and in the Hebrides or Sudreys, which means southern isles in the Norse language.

There are three kinds of evidence about the Viking presence in Scotland.

Archaeology

Many sites of Viking graves have been found. The goods which were buried alongside the bodies give us a lot of information about Viking life, such as what they used for cooking and other everyday activities and what goods they traded.

The Norse stories/sagas

These sagas were originally told as stories and written down later. They concentrate on telling of heroic deeds of warriors, but also mention many places in Scotland.

Place name evidence

Many Scottish towns and areas are named from Viking words which indicate that Vikings settled there. The box below shows some of the prefixes and suffixes to place names which come from the Viking language.

Viking Word	Meaning
ness	a head of land
vik or wick	a bay or harbour
ay or say	an island
bster, bister or bost	a farm
dale	a valley
howe	a mound
by or bie	a town

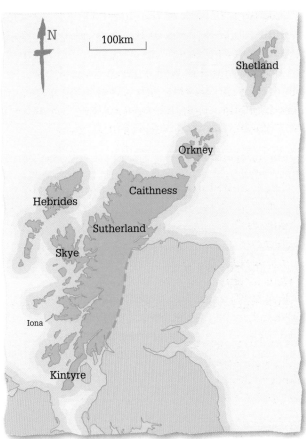

Areas of Viking settlements in Scotland.

Questions

1. When did the Vikings begin to settle in Scotland and where did they settle first?

Extension task

1. Copy the table of Viking words and their meanings into your workbook. Then, using a map of Scotland, find five examples of place names. Remember – many of them will be the endings of places, for example, Inverness. Write your answer as a table with the following headings:

Viking word	Meaning	Example

The Vikings as traders and farmers

The Vikings did not only influence life in Scotland. Vikings from Denmark also conquered large parts of England, particularly in the north and east. This area was sometimes called the Danelaw. Vikings from both Norway and Denmark attacked Ireland as well, known throughout Europe in the eighth century as a centre of Christian learning. Later, they began to settle there permanently. They sometimes ranged even further, down the coast of France and eastwards into what is now Russia.

Traditional stories tell of Viking cruelty and slaughter. However, historians have revised these views as more evidence has been found. A lot of this new evidence shows that in the places where Vikings settled, they brought with them many skills apart from fighting and seafaring. One such place was the Viking village of Jarlshof in Shetland. This was a farming community, where there was enough land to grow crops and rear sheep, providing a better living than in Norway.

The Vikings were also traders. Swedish archaeologists have shown that the town of Visby on the Baltic Sea was a huge trading centre, linking Scandinavia not just with Russia to the east and the British Isles to the west, but also with the Mediterranean Sea and the Middle East. Scottish finds such as the Skaill hoard (Source E), discovered in Orkney, also show evidence of this overseas trade.

14

Aerial photograph of Jarlshof. ▼

Source D

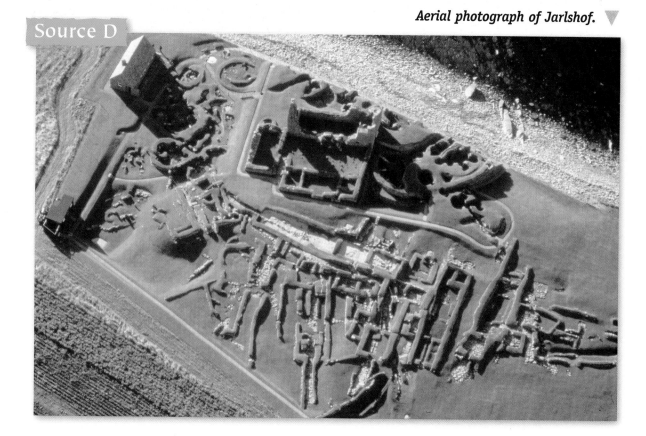

In a period of over 500 years, thousands of Vikings settled in Scotland and their way of life and beliefs changed. From being feared as the pagan raiders who destroyed monasteries and slaughtered innocent people, they became peaceful, Christian farmers and fishermen. They mixed with the local people and intermarried with them. Some of them spent some of their leisure time playing games such as chess. We know this as the famous Lewis chess pieces (Source F) date from the twelfth century, when the Hebrides were still ruled by Norway.

Source E

Arabic coins from the Skaill hoard. ▲

Source F

Three of the Lewis chess pieces, made from ivory. ▲

15

Questions

1. Where, apart from Scotland, did Vikings settle?

2. Why is Source E useful as evidence that the Vikings were not simply warriors?

By the 840s, the Picts and the Scots were ruled by one king. The people of **Alba** (Scotia in Latin), as the kingdom was known, spoke the Gaelic of the Scots rather than Pictish. The two centuries until about 1050 were times of great violence. The kings of Alba had to fight against invaders from Scandinavia, Ireland and England. There were also many challenges to their authority from powerful men within their kingdom. Many kings of Alba died violent deaths, being murdered or killed in battle. The kings of Alba ruled the area north of the rivers Forth and Clyde, but also had to fight against increasing Viking attacks in the north and west and invading Angles to the south.

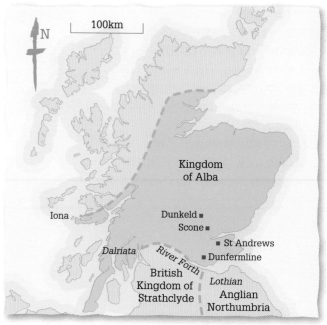

The Kingdom of Alba.

The Alban kings

The first king of the Picts and Scots was Kenneth MacAlpin, who was a Scot (Gael) from Dalriata. He may not have been the first Scottish king to rule the Picts, but he moved the centre of power from Dalriata to Scone in Pictland. This may have been to escape Viking attacks. Two other important kings of Alba were Constantine II (900–943) who despite losing an important battle against the Angles, strengthened Alba by building an alliance with the Vikings, and pushing south into Lothian to conquer more land. He eventually gave up his throne to become a monk at St Andrews. Malcolm II (1005–34), allied with King Owen of Strathclyde, defeated the Angles in 1018 at the Battle of Carham near Kelso in the borders. The whole of Lothian was now under the rule of the MacAlpin kings. When Owen died shortly after the Battle of Carham, Malcolm made his grandson Duncan ruler of Strathclyde. Duncan succeeded his grandfather as king of Alba in 1034. Alba was now looking very like modern Scotland.

The Alban kings made several important changes which laid the foundations of the kingdom of Scotland.

- The royal centre moved from Dalriata to Perthshire in the east.
- St Andrews in Fife and Dunkeld in Perthshire replaced Iona as the most important religious centres.

Source A

Kenneth MacAlpin, as portrayed by a sixteenth-century artist.

- Kings were now crowned at Scone near Perth. The Stone of Destiny, on which they sat to be crowned, was moved to Scone so that it could be used in the crowning ceremony.
- Most of southern Scotland became part of Alba.
- The Picts disappeared as a separate people. Although their distinctive stones were still made, their language died out at around this time.

The kings of Alba

Kenneth MacAlpin	843–858	Culen	966–971
Donald I	858–862	Kenneth II	971–975
Constantine I	862–877	Constantine III	995–997
Aed	877–878	Kenneth III	997–1005
Eochaid	878–889	Malcolm II	1005–1034
Donald II	889–900	Duncan I	1034–1040
Constantine II	903–943	Macbeth	1040–1057
Malcom I	943–954	Lulach	1057–1058
Indulf	954–962	Malcolm III	1058–1093
Dubh	962–966	Donald Bane	1093–1097

Malcolm and Margaret (1058–93)

In 1058, Malcolm Canmore became king of Scots after a four-year struggle against King Macbeth and his son Lulach. (In Gaelic 'ceann mor', where his name comes from, means great head or chief.) Malcolm was the son of Duncan, who had been deposed by Macbeth in 1040. He married Margaret in 1070 and the couple made Scotland a more outward-looking country.

Malcolm had spent fourteen years in exile in Northumbria, and grew up speaking English and French as well as Gaelic. He spent much of his reign trying to add northern England to his kingdom, without much success. Malcolm moved the centre of power from Perthshire to the Lowlands, building a new stronghold at Dunfermline and reinforcing the defences of Edinburgh.

17

Source B

A sixteenth-century painting of Malcolm and Margaret.

In 1066, the Normans invaded England and defeated and killed King Harold at the Battle of Hastings. Several important English people then fled to Scotland as refugees to escape from the Normans, including Margaret. Her brother was Edgar Atheling, who claimed the English throne. Margaret was born in Hungary but had been brought up in England. Well-educated and very religious even by the standards of the time, she was a complete contrast to her husband (see Source C).

Source C

Turgot describes how she supported 24 poor people all year round, ministered daily to nine abandoned orphans, washed the feet of six of the poor during the seasons of Lent and Advent and had 300 more fed in the royal hall before herself.

An extract from a modern history book written in 1992. (Turgot was Margaret's friend and priest. He later wrote her life story and became bishop of St Andrews.)

Margaret brought many new ideas to Scotland. According to Turgot, she wanted to change how the Church in Scotland was run. The mass, or church service, was brought into line with the rest of Europe and Sunday was reserved for rest and worship – no work was to be done. Margaret set up a ferry across the River Forth to make it easier for pilgrims to reach the shrine of St Andrew. This was soon called the Queen's Ferry. She also invited English monks to start a priory at Dunfermline, the first of many new monastic foundations in Scotland. She had her own chapel built on Edinburgh's castle rock, where it still stands today, the oldest surviving building in Edinburgh.

The era of Malcolm and Margaret was a bridge between the Celtic Scotland of the Kingdom of Alba and the newer world of the Normans to the south. Despite the hostility between the royal couple and the conquerors of England, Norman influences grew, as we will see in the next chapter.

18

Source D

▲ *St Margaret's Chapel, Edinburgh Castle.*

Questions

1. Why was the period between 840 and 1050 a violent time?

2. In what ways did the kings of Alba make their kingdom more like modern Scotland?

3. Look at Source C and the text below it. Does this explain why Margaret became known later as St Margaret?

Extension task

1. Using the school library, the local library or the Internet, find out more about:

   a. The Kingdom of Alba

   b. Malcolm and Margaret.

   Write a report on your findings.

5 David I and the feudal system

The Normans invaded England in 1066. They were a warlike people who were the descendants of Viking settlers in France. After decades of raiding the coasts and rivers of France, these Northmen were granted land in the north-west of the country. This area of France is still called Normandy – the land of the Northmen or Vikings.

Normandy and the British Isles.

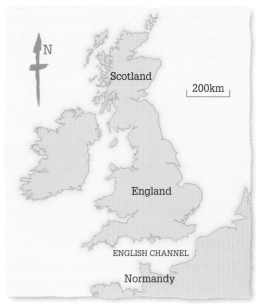

When the English king, Edward the Confessor died early in 1066, Harold Godwinson became king. Although Edward had named Harold as his heir (he had no children), there were several other men who claimed the English throne, including the Viking Harald Hardrada and William, Duke of Normandy. Harold defeated a Viking invasion in September 1066 at the Battle of Stamford Bridge, but then had to return south quickly to deal with the Normans, who had landed on the south coast. On 14 October 1066, the English army was defeated by the Normans at the Battle of Hastings. Harold was killed, and on Christmas Day, William of Normandy was crowned King of England in London.

The feudal system comes to Scotland

Over the next few years, William and his supporters conquered the rest of England, despite several rebellions. To control his new kingdom, William established the feudal system. Less than a century after this, King David I of Scots started to bring the feudal system to Scotland. As a young man, David had lived in England where he owned large estates, and had many Norman friends. When he became King of Scots in 1124, David decided to try to make Scotland into a feudal country. He invited many of his Norman friends to Scotland to help him defeat his enemies and to change the way the country was run. Many took up David's offer and were rewarded with land.

The feudal system was all about land. King David owned the whole of Scotland, but put most of it in the care of his Norman barons. They were called his **vassals**. In return for this land, the barons (or nobles) promised to obey the king, who was their superior. The barons also had to supply the king with a number of knights. The king also granted land to the Church.

The lands held in this way were called **fiefs**. Most barons kept some land for themselves, but rented much of it out to their tenants. This process of giving out fiefs was made legal by a royal charter. The charter was written in Latin on a piece of parchment. Latin was the language used in most countries of Europe in the Middle Ages for writing important documents.

At the bottom of the charter were the names of several people who were witnesses to the charter. The king's seal was stamped on wax and fixed to the bottom right-hand corner of the charter. The baron would lock the charter away safely, because this was the evidence which proved that the land belonged to him.

Source A

David, by the Grace of God, King of the Scots does hereby give to his faithful servant, Robert Bruce all the lands of the Lordship of Annandale; to include all the fields, forests, meadows, rivers, houses, mills and all other things within the Lordship. Also Robert is given the castle of Lochmaben which is to be the centre of the Lordship. IN RETURN, Robert will provide ten knights, fully armed and with a good horse, to fight in the army of the king when called upon to do so. If Robert should not provide the said ten knights, his lands will be taken away from him. LIST OF WITNESSES: Duncan Earl of Fife, Richard Comyn, William Somerville, Walter Stewart, Geoffrey Melville. This charter is written by the hand of our Chancellor in the year of our Lord, 1124 David R.

Charter granting lands of Annandale to Robert Bruce.

Questions

1. Why is a charter like the one in Source A a useful source for an historian of the Middle Ages? To answer this question properly, we can break it down as follows. All these points should be included in your answer:

   a. When was the charter made? Was this during the Middle Ages?

   b. Who actually wrote the charter?

   c. What does the charter tell us?

   d. Why was the charter written? You might need to refer back to the text to answer this question.

Extension task

1. Now think of a friend to whom you would like to give a piece of land. Make your own feudal charter granting your friend the fief. At the bottom of the charter you should add the signatures of three or four of your friends. Then make a drawing of the kind of seal you would like to have had if you had been the king. This should be placed in the right hand bottom corner of your charter.

The reign of David I (1124–53): Monasteries, castles and burghs

David I was a very important king in Scotland's history. Many of the things we take for granted today developed during his reign. He brought many new ideas to Scotland, but kept some of the old traditions of the Kingdom of Alba.

As well as granting land to Norman barons, David gave some of his royal lands to religious orders of the Church. Several monasteries were built as a result of this, including Kelso, Melrose and Dryburgh in the Borders. There was a growth in towns and trade during his reign; fifteen burghs (trading centres) were founded. David also began the first standard coinage (money) which helped trade to grow. Another important feature of David's reign was the development of castles. All the barons who were granted land built themselves strong castles for protection, to defend their land and as living accommodation.

David's reign also brought conflict with England, despite the close relationship between the two royal families. David had land in England granted to him by King Henry I, so when Henry's daughter Maud was deposed as queen of England by Stephen, her uncle David raised an army to support her. He also wanted to extend his kingdom further south to include Northumberland and Cumbria. However, David's army was defeated in 1138 at the Battle of the Standard in North Yorkshire. Fortunately, Stephen (the English king) was content with saving the north of his kingdom from Scots invasion and when a peace treaty was agreed the next year, David was able to hold on to Cumbria and Northumberland.

Source B

▲ *David I (left) and his grandson Malcolm IV.*

David was middle-aged when he became king, so it was surprising that he ruled for nearly 30 years. He died at Carlisle in 1153, and was buried at Dunfermline Abbey. His only son and heir, Henry, died the year before, so he was succeeded by his grandson Malcom IV. No other king before David had such an impact on Scotland.

Questions

1. When did David I become king and what new ideas did he introduce to Scotland?

2. Look at Source B. This one of the first pictures we have of Scottish kings. Try to work out what this source can tell us about kings in the twelfth century. Consider:

   ● How they are dressed
   ● What they are holding
   ● What they are sitting on.

6 Castles

When the Normans came to England, one of the first things they did was to build castles. These strongholds were built by the barons to dominate the area which they ruled. When David I introduced the feudal system to Scotland, the Norman barons started to build castles.

Motte and bailey castles

The earliest castles in Scotland were built in the north-east and south-west of the country. These areas had always been difficult for kings to control, so the Norman barons who built the castles were expected to help David I in this task. The first castles were made of earth, turf and timber, and are known as **motte and bailey** castles. The motte was a steep mound of earth (which could be dug very quickly) or a glacial mound. The wooden stronghold was built on top of the motte and surrounded by a wooden fence or palisade. The bailey was where the other castle buildings were – kitchens, stables, barns and sometimes a chapel. The bailey was also surrounded by a wall and the entire structure was often enclosed by a ditch.

▲ *The Motte of Urr, Kirkcudbright.*

From these strongholds, the Norman barons could keep control of their lands. Rent and food were collected from the local people, with the threat of force if necessary. Nowadays, there are few visible remains of motte and bailey castles and only the mottes can sometimes be seen.

◀ *A typical motte and bailey castle.*

Stone castles

In time, as technology and building skills developed, motte and bailey castles were replaced by castles made of stone. These were much more difficult for enemies to attack and capture, mainly because it was impossible to set fire to them. Today, the remains of medieval stone castles can be seen in most parts of Scotland. Castle building became very important, especially for kings, and the structures became more complicated over the years. Castles were also homes for families and not just strongholds.

An artist's reconstruction of the concentric castle at Dundonald.

The first stone castles were called shell keeps, because the wall was like a shell. These keeps were built on the top of the motte, replacing the wooden tower. One problem with the motte and bailey castle had been that the area on top of the motte was very small so there was little living space. Later keeps became too large to be built on a motte, so were placed inside the bailey, which was level. The wooden fence surrounding the bailey was replaced by one made of stone. This was called a curtain wall. Barons made their curtain walls stronger by building towers. The entrance to the castle was still in the wall, but was usually built inside a stone gatehouse with towers on either side. Castle windows were narrow slits designed to prevent attackers climbing in, but arrows could be fired through them from the inside. Higher up the walls of the keep the windows became larger.

Castles in the thirteenth century became very sophisticated. Examples of these castles with concentric towers can still be seen at Dirleton in East Lothian and Bothwell in Lanarkshire. Recent excavations at Dundonald castle in Ayrshire have uncovered another concentric castle, replacing an earlier motte and bailey structure (Source B). Alexander Stewart was one of the most powerful barons in thirteenth century Scotland. He had seen the famous French castle at Coucy and was inspired to have something similar built when he returned to Scotland. Dundonald was very much a state-of-the-art castle.

Questions

1. Where and why were the first castles in Scotland built?

2. Describe the main features of a motte and bailey castle. You may include a sketch in your answer.

3. Why is there so little evidence about motte and bailey castles?

4. What type of castle replaced motte and bailey castles and why?

5. Give an example of this new type of castle and describe it.

Attacking and defending a castle

Castles were essential for controlling the surrounding lands. With entrances high above ground level and thick walls, they were very difficult to capture. Most attackers realised this, so usually tried to surround the castle and starve out the defenders. This was called a **siege**. The siege could take months, so the attackers would try to capture the castle by force. The two main methods used were tunnelling under the walls, or using siege engines (see below) to damage or get over the castle walls. Tunnelling was dangerous and often not successful. The tunnellers usually tried to set fire to the walls above their tunnel, but this became harder once castles were stone-built. Tunnels could also sometimes collapse.

▲ *A siege in progress.*

Many of the siege engines used by attackers had not changed much since they were used in Roman times.

- A wooden siege-tower or belfry was built high enough to reach the top of the castle walls, while other attackers used scaling ladders to climb up the walls.
- A giant crossbow or ballista was used to fire large arrows.
- Mangonels and trebuchets were stone-throwing machines or catapults, which were used to make holes in the castle walls and let the attackers in or to injure defenders inside the castle.
- A battering ram was used to attack the gatehouse or main entrance of the castle. The ram was made from tree trunks.

When Edward I of England besieged Stirling Castle in 1304, it took him three months to capture it, despite using thirteen siege-engines, including his 'war-wolf'. This engine was designed to throw stones which weighed over 100 kilograms.

Living in a castle

Castles were also homes to the baron, his family and his servants. Every castle had several floors, each with its own toilet or **garderobe**. At the top were the battlements where soldiers patrolled along the wall-walk. Below the battlements were the bedrooms, usually at the top of the gatehouse. However, barons later had their bedrooms in more private parts of the castle. The Great Hall was a long, bare room with large windows to let in as much light as possible (Source C). Here, the baron got on with the daily business of running his estates and at night held banquets. Often, window seats were built into the walls and there were galleries where musicians would entertain the baron and his guests. The walls were sometimes hung with tapestries.

Every castle had large kitchens, often near the Great Hall. They had large open fires and ovens, all built into the thick walls. There would also be a pantry for storing food, a buttery for bottles, a bakehouse and a brewhouse for making beer. Every castle had a well, which ensured a regular water supply, especially when under siege. Because religion played such an important part in people's lives in the Middle Ages, every castle had a chapel. This was near the baron's own private rooms, and was usually rich in religious paintings and decorated stonework – paid for by the baron. The different floors of the castle were connected by spiral staircases built round the corners of the towers.

Source C

▲ *The Great Hall at Stirling Castle.*

Questions

1. What were the two main methods used to try to capture a castle?

2. Why was the Great Hall the most important room in a castle?

3. What were the different parts of the kitchen?

4. Why do you think the baron spent a lot of money on the chapel?

In the Middle Ages, the Christian Church was very important in the lives of most people. On pages 7–9 you saw how Christianity came to Scotland, and how the Roman rules were adopted in place of Celtic rules. By the twelfth century, kings such as David I needed the support of the Church, which was headed by the Pope in Rome. The Church also relied on kings for many things too. Kings showed their power by endowing monasteries or paying for elaborate decorations in churches. The best educated people in Scotland were Churchmen.

Parishes and priests

By the time of David I (1124), Scotland was covered by a network of parishes, each with a parish church built of stone. They were usually built by the local people. Some of Scotland's earliest surviving churches date from this time. The ceremonies of baptism, marriage and burial were carried out by the priest, as well as the mass or religious service. People were fined if they did not go to church regularly and obey its laws.

The parish priest, or rector, was often as poor as his parishioners. Every family was supposed to pay a tenth of their income (a **tithe**) to the Church. Part of this went to pay the rector, but often he was simply given food instead. Sometimes he would have some farm land beside the church. This was called the **glebe**.

Source A

▲ *Dalmeny church.*

Bishops and cathedrals

Parishes were grouped together geographically into a **diocese**. A bishop, often appointed by the king, was in charge of the diocese. The centre of the diocese was a large church called a cathedral. In most countries, an archbishop was in charge of the bishops, but Scotland did not have one. The English Archbishop of York claimed to be head of the Scottish Church, but the bishops disagreed. This caused a lot of arguments. The most important Scottish Churchman was the Bishop of St Andrews in Fife. Thousands of pilgrims came to the town to pray at the shrine of St Andrew. In the twelfth century, the bishop began the building of a cathedral, which became the largest in Scotland. Bishops and other Churchmen often helped the king to govern his lands. Highly educated, they were often the sons of wealthy parents.

The dioceses of Scotland in the Middle Ages. ▶

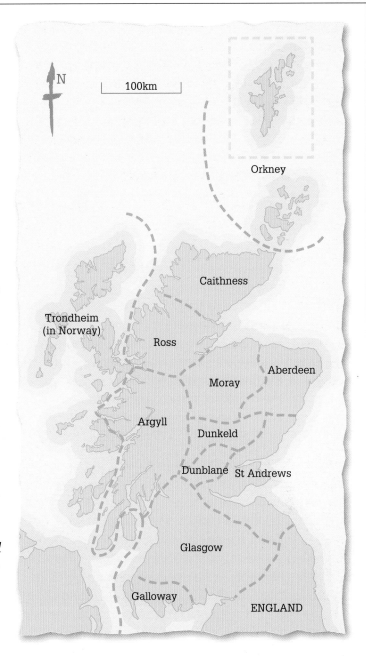

Monks, monasteries and abbeys

Monks, like priests, devoted their lives to the service of God. They spent most of their lives with other monks in religious communities called **monasteries** or **abbeys**. Queen Margaret and King David I both gave money to set up new abbeys. The ruins of several abbeys can still be seen in many parts of Scotland, especially in the Borders. Abbeys were usually built in isolated places, but often had excellent farmland. This was so that the monks could supply all the food they needed. Wealthy barons, merchants and even kings sometimes made gifts of land and buildings to the monks. Abbeys were great landowners and rented out some of their lands, which brought them even more wealth.

Source B

I David, by the Grace of God King of Scots, at God's prompting and for the benefit of my soul have founded a monastery in the town of Jedburgh in which I have established canons regular. To provide for them I give and confirm by this my charter, the monastery of Jedburgh with everything in it and the tithes of the villages of the parish. Also a tenth of the income from my forest of Teviotdale and the right to graze animals near my woodlands and take timber from my woods. Also payment from the people of Jedburgh for grinding corn at the abbey mill.

Extract from Royal Charter of David I to the monastery at Jedburgh, 1147.

Monks belonged to different orders. Queen Margaret had invited the Benedictine order to Dunfermline in 1070, and others followed. This was part of a Europe-wide revival of monasticism. The Benedictine order was the most important religious order, but other orders became increasingly important such as Cistercians, Carthusians and Augustinians. Each order was made up of canons, who were more like priests, and monks. David I invited canons of the Augustinian order to start Jedburgh Abbey. Historians believe these canons lived like monks. The Cistercian order founded the abbeys of Melrose in the Borders and Dundrennan in Galloway, also during the reign of David I. The monks of these orders all took solemn vows (promises) to obey God and the rules of the Church (obedience), not to have any personal wealth (poverty) and not to marry (chastity).

Different orders had different routines, but a monk's daily routine was very strict. It did not vary much from day to day, starting very early in the morning with the first of seven church services, called **Matins**. Apart from meals and services, a monk's day was spent working. They did different jobs. Those with good handwriting would work as scribes, copying and decorating manuscripts on to sheets of parchment (thick paper), using a quill pen. Other jobs were done on the abbey's lands or helping to run the various functions of the abbey, such as assisting the Infirmarian, who looked after the sick, the Almoner, who gave food to the poor or the Hospitaller, who gave travellers accommodation for the night.

Nuns and friars

Nowadays there are a lot of arguments in the different Christian Churches about the place of women. Some Churches have women priests and ministers, others do not. In the Middle Ages, women who wanted to devote their lives to serve the Church had much less choice than men. If a woman did not want to stay at home, marry and bring up children, her only other real choice was to become a nun. Nuns took similar vows to monks, devoting their lives to God, and lived together in nunneries or priories, which were run along the same lines as monasteries. The two main differences were that the head of the nunnery was usually a man, the Prior,

Source C

▲ *Nuns in the Middle Ages.*

Source D

29

A Dominican Friar. ▷

and that the nuns were not supposed to do hard manual work. They still cooked, cleaned and worked in the fields or attended to the sick. Sometimes very wealthy women who had been widowed gave up all their possessions to become nuns. As monks and nuns were often very well educated, some orders encouraged them to teach.

Friars also dedicated their lives to God, but did not live in one place. Mostly, they travelled around the country preaching to the people and begging from them. This was because they were supposed to live in absolute poverty. Friars usually had a base in one of the towns, called a friary. Towns had big enough populations to support begging and sometimes a wealthy person would give the friars a place to build a friary. In some ways these were similar in design and layout to monasteries.

There were several different orders of friars. The most important were the Carmelites or White Friars (so called because they wore a white robe or habit) the Dominicans or Black Friars and the Franciscans or Grey Friars. Dominicans were widely known for their interest in education, and set up schools in many places.

Education

Nearly all schools in Scotland in the Middle Ages were run by the Church. This was because all priests and nuns had to have a good education to carry out their duties properly and so could read and write. The Church also needed men and women with specialist knowledge of the law and of the Bible and other religious works to continue the education of the monks and nuns.

All teachers were members of the Church. Most schools were in towns or monasteries and were for boys only. They were called grammar schools, because the main subject taught was Latin grammar. Latin was the international language of the Church, and was used for all its business in every country of Europe. Sometimes a wealthy person gave money to their local grammar school to help educate poor boys who showed promise.

There were no universities in Scotland until the fifteenth century, so further study after leaving school was only possible by going to Oxford or Cambridge in England, Paris or Orleans in France, Louvain in Flanders (Belgium), Cologne in Germany or Padua in Italy.

Questions

1. Look at the map showing the dioceses of Scotland. Who controls all of the islands? Can you think why?

2. Look at Source B. David I made sure that Jedburgh Abbey would be well provided for. How did he do this?

3. What differences were there between the lives of nuns and monks in the Middle Ages?

4. a. Explain the difference between a monk and a friar.
   b. Why did friars beg?
   c. What were the three main orders of friars and how did they get their names?

5. a. Why were schools in the Middle Ages run by the Church?
   b. What was the main subject taught and why?
   c. Why did talented scholars go outside Scotland for further study?

Extension tasks

1. Describe a typical day in the life of a monk. You may wish to use extra resources from your school library, resource centre or the Internet.

2. Is there a church or other religious building dating from the Middle Ages in your area? Try to find out as much information as you can about it from your school resource centre or local library.

Life in the countryside

In medieval Scotland, more than 90 per cent of the population lived and worked on the land. By modern standards, farming was a hard life. Compared to England and France, Scotland was a poor country. Unlike its two larger neighbours, Scotland did not have any large areas of good farmland and the climate was harsher. Life was a constant struggle to survive. Most people in the countryside grew enough food for themselves but had little left over. If the crops failed one year, there could be famine.

The ferm toun

Farmers in most parts of lowland Scotland lived in rural settlements called ferm touns. They were not really like modern villages. The ferm toun was home for between four and eight families. These families rented their land from the local baron or abbot of a monastery, or perhaps the king. The farmers had to pay rent to this superior in money or kind (goods/produce) and also had to work for him.

A ferm toun. ▼

We know very little about the houses of the people who lived in ferm touns, as none has survived, even as ruins. Much of the evidence is hidden in the modern landscape of the countryside. Local materials were used by farmers to build their homes, usually wood and stone. They were called **long houses** and had an earth floor and a hearth or fireplace in the middle of the living area. The smoke from the fire escaped through a hole in the roof. One part of the house was called the byre and this was where the animals were kept. The roof had a wooden frame, with a layer of turf and a thatch of heather, ferns or rushes. Windows were just small holes in the walls, and doors were made of wicker covered in animal skins. There was little furniture – perhaps a table, a couple of stools and a storage chest. Beds were box-like and had mattresses of straw, heather or bracken.

Infield and outfield

In most ferm touns, there was only a small area of land for growing crops (arable land). This area was usually nearest to the toun and was called the infield. The outfield was further away from the toun. It was rough, stony ground and was used for grazing animals. The infield was divided into long strip fields or rigs. Each rig was the size of land that could be ploughed in a day, and would be about 4.5 metres long. The crops were grown on the rigs and there was a ditch or baulk between each rig.

Source A

Aerial photograph of rigs in Aberdeenshire.

Nobody had the same rigs for long. Each family had several rigs scattered over the infield and every spring they would draw lots for their rigs. This was to make sure that every family got a fair share of the good, fertile land as well as the not-so-good land. The system was called **run-rig**.

Questions

1. Make a list of all the differences between the house you live in and a long house. Think of construction materials, number of rooms, windows, heating, furniture, beds.

2. Explain the following words: arable, infield, outfield, rigs.

Extended writing

1. 'A fair but inefficient way of farming'. What evidence can you find in this section to support this statement about the run-rig system?

Crops and livestock

To survive, farming families hoped for good weather at the right time of year, just like farmers today. Because it was expensive to drain land, much of the arable land was higher up than nowadays. This ensured that rainwater would run off naturally down the slopes. The only fertiliser farmers used was human or animal manure.

Source B

Ane tae saw
Ane tae gnaw
And ane tae pay the laird witha
An old Scots verse.

33

For every ear of grain planted, farmers could only expect three or four back, one of which had to be kept for sowing the next spring. The most common crops grown were oats and barley, with some wheat, mainly in the south-east, where the climate was drier. Wheaten bread was really only eaten by the wealthy, most people ate oatmeal, porridge, oat cakes and barley-broth. They drank ale made from barley. Root crops like potatoes and turnips were unknown.

Cattle and sheep were the most common animals in the ferm toun. Sheep provided mutton and wool and in many cases, milk. Wool was used to make clothes and was exported to England or Flanders. Cattle were kept for their meat and hides, which were made into leather. Milk from cattle, goats and sheep was made into cheese or butter. Pigs were also kept in large numbers for their meat. Even the poorest farmers grazed pigs in the woods around the ferm toun, feeding them on acorns and beech-mast. Fish was also eaten, caught from nearby rivers or ponds, or the sea if the ferm toun was near the coast.

Source C

Alexander ... King of Scots ... has decided that all men living in farms and touns during the past year must begin to plough and sow with all their might ... Also that a man who has more than 4 cattle shall rent land from his lord and shall plough and sow to feed his family. A man who has less than 5 cattle, and cannot plough with oxen, shall with their hands and feet delve the earth. Any lord who will not allow this in his lands shall pay a fine of 8 cattle to the king.
Royal law of 1214 ordering more land to be ploughed.

Tools and the farmer's year

Medieval farmers in Scotland used a heavy wooden plough to prepare the land for sowing. Up to eight oxen and four men were needed to operate this and it took a day to plough half an acre, about half a football pitch. This was roughly the area of one rig. The only metal part of the plough was the blade or coulter, which dug into the soil. However, the **coulter** did not cut a very deep furrow (trench), so that weeds and stones would sometimes be left. In some areas, especially in the Highlands, the land was too rough for a plough to be used. Here, the land would have to be delved (dug) using a **cas-chrom** (crooked spade). With its triangular blade, the cas-chrom could turn over the soil quite deeply. After ploughing, the farmers scattered the grain seeds by hand, walking up and down the rigs. A harrow was used to press the seeds into the soil and cover them up.

A cas-chrom. ▲

At harvest time, the crops were cut (reaped) with a sickle. Everybody was needed to help with the harvest. The cut corn was tied together in stooks, then threshed to separate the grain from the stalks. This was a demanding task, using tools called flails. After threshing, the corn was winnowed to separate the ears from the loose husks. This was usually done outside when there was a strong wind, because the breeze blew away the loose husks.

Most of the corn was then taken to the local water-mill for processing into flour or malt for ale. The mill was owned by the local baron, who charged a high fee for the use of the mill, although farmers often blamed the miller (the person who operated the mill) for the high prices.

Questions

1. Read Source B. Try to work out what the verse means. You may need a dictionary to help. How accurate is Source B about Scottish farming in the Middle Ages?

2. Read Source C. Why do you think Scottish kings sometimes ordered people to plough more land?

3. Why was a cas-chrom sometimes used instead of a plough?

4. Why was it important that everybody in the ferm toun helped at harvest time? Use the text to help with your answer.

34

Towns and trade

Towns in Scotland first sprang up because people needed to trade; farmers wanted to exchange the surplus food they had grown for clothes. To begin with, trading places were very small, but they soon grew. During the reign of David I most of these trading towns were made into royal **burghs**. This meant that they had been granted a charter by the king, giving the merchants who lived there certain privileges.

The layout of a burgh

Burghs were usually located near a castle and a river crossing or estuary for good trade links. The buildings were surrounded by a wooden wall and deep ditch for defence. People could only enter through stone gateways in the walls called ports. There were one or two main streets, one usually called the High Street or Gait. The houses were built of wood and stood with their gable-ends (sides) facing the street. There was a long narrow piece of land behind each house, called a toft or backland, where the townsman and his family would have workshops, stables and sheds. In the centre of the main street stood the market (mercat) cross, which was the focus of burgh life. People would gather here to listen to travelling friars or to the Town Crier reading important announcements. It was also where law-breakers were dealt with, but most importantly, the weekly market was held here.

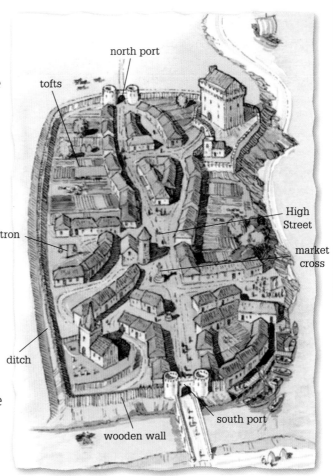

A typical medieval burgh.

35

Royal burghs

Royal burghs were started by David I (1124–53). The evidence in Source A gives us some idea of the importance of burghs.

Privileges were often very detailed. Kings were frequent visitors to royal burghs, so there was usually a royal residence and sometimes a mint (a place where coins were made). The use of coins helped trade to grow. There were three mints in Scotland by the end of David I's reign at Berwick, Roxburgh and Edinburgh. By the middle of the thirteenth century, more coins were being minted.

Source A

Within the Sheriffdom of Lanark, no one may buy wool or hides or any other goods, or make broad cloth, except the merchants of Lanark. Any stranger merchant who tries to come into this Sheriffdom to buy wool, hides or similar merchandise shall be seized along with his goods.

The rights of the burgh of Lanark, Alexander III, 1285.

This was done mainly at Berwick, which was by far the largest burgh in Scotland in the Middle Ages, and had a large overseas trade.

When David I died in 1153, there were sixteen royal burghs. More burghs were granted privileges by his successors. By 1286, there were 27, and other towns had been granted charters by barons or the Church.

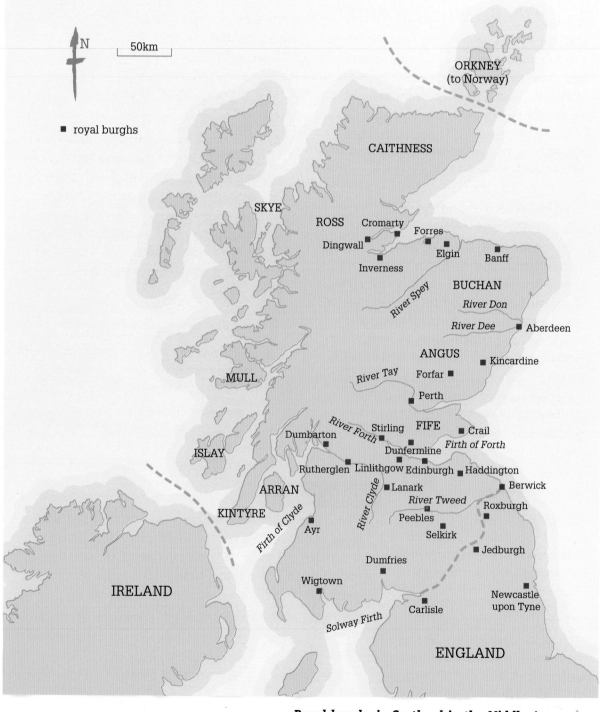

N

50km

■ royal burghs

ORKNEY
(to Norway)

CAITHNESS

SKYE

ROSS   Cromarty
              Forres
Dingwall   Elgin   Banff
      Inverness

BUCHAN

River Spey

River Don

River Dee   Aberdeen

ANGUS   Kincardine

River Tay   Forfar

MULL   Perth

River Forth   Stirling   FIFE   Crail
Dumbarton   Firth of Forth
                Dunfermline
ISLAY
        Rutherglen   Linlithgow   Edinburgh   Haddington
ARRAN   Lanark   Berwick
KINTYRE   River Tweed   Roxburgh
                    Peebles
        Ayr   Selkirk
                        Jedburgh
IRELAND   Dumfries
        Wigtown   Newcastle
                upon Tyne
            Carlisle

Firth of Clyde
River Clyde

Solway Firth

ENGLAND

Royal burghs in Scotland in the Middle Ages. ▲

Merchants and craftsmen

The merchants of the burgh (burgesses) were the only people allowed to trade inside the burgh and with foreign merchants. They ran the affairs of the burgh through its council. There were usually about twelve councillors, elected by the burgesses. The Provost was the leader. He was helped by two bailies, who acted as judges in the burgh court.

The burgesses who sat on the council were also members of another very important organisation, the Merchant Guild. Members who broke the rules of the Guild could be fined. Guild members from other burghs could only trade with merchants, not the public. Anybody from another burgh was a 'foreigner' and was only allowed to stay for one night. Source B shows that guilds like Berwick's made laws for many things apart from trade.

Source B

We order that no one dare place filth, dust or ashes on the street, or in the market-place, or on the banks of the river Tweed, as this could hurt or damage passers-by. If anyone does so, he shall be fined eight shillings.

Extract from laws of the Berwick Guild.

There were many craftsmen in the burgh. Men employed in the same craft usually lived in the same street. These craftsmen mainly processed the products of the countryside – wool, cattle meat and hides, and corn or flour. A local farmer might sell his cow at the market to a flesher, who would then slaughter the cow.

Both merchants and craftsmen lived in houses above their workplaces. A painted sign above the workshop indicated what craft was being carried out. Each craftsman worked with a journeyman, fully qualified in his trade, and several apprentices who were learning th craft. The journeyman was paid a small wage, living with his master until he could afford to get married anc get his own house. He hoped one day to be his own master and have his own workshop. This could only happen if he produced his 'master's piece' to demonstrate to the other craftsmen that he was good enough to join them.

Source C

The corpse of the cow would be divided into meat, brains, hide, hoof and horn, for every part was useful. Dealing with the hide was as urgent as selling the meat. Otherwise it would rot.

A quote from a modern historian.

Markets

The market was held every week. Country people living near the burgh came to sell their produce. They would then buy goods which they did not produce themselves, such as salt, nails or maybe a new blade for the plough. The area in the centre of the burgh around the market cross would be very crowded, with many stalls. The merchants had strict rules about the market to make sure that nobody was cheated. Prices were fixed so that traders could not make massive profits by charging high prices, or take away other traders' business by setting low prices. Although there was no agreed system of weights and measures for all Scotland, all goods had to be weighed at the public weighing beam, or Tron.

Nowadays fast transport and communication enable people to buy and sell goods outside Scotland and trade has become international. In the Middle Ages, trade was much more difficult as the only means of transport were road and water. Roads were simply dirt tracks, so moving goods was slow and time consuming. This made any goods carried by horse and cart more than a short distance very expensive. Long distance trade, even within Scotland, went by water. This is why so many burghs were situated on the coast or at river estuaries or crossing points. **Imports** (goods coming into a country) and **exports** (goods going out of a country) were all carried by ship. This could be dangerous, as a ship might get wrecked in a storm or captured by pirates. However, merchants involved in overseas trade were willing to take such risks because the potential profits were huge.

Many of the goods brought back to Scotland by these ships would be sold at the annual fair. Also, foreign merchants came to the fair with even more exotic and luxury items for sale, such as rich cloth from Flanders, soft leather from Italy and even spices and herbs from Asia. For most ordinary people who could not afford to buy expensive goods like these, the fair provided entertainment such as jugglers, acrobats, wrestlers and dancing bears.

Questions

1. Look at Source A. What privileges do the merchants of Lanark have?

2. Where was Scotland's largest town in the Middle Ages? Can you think of anything unusual about this?

3. Look at Source B. What problem is the merchant guild of Berwick trying to deal with?

4. Look at the list of craftsmen below. Try to describe what they did. You may need a dictionary to help.

- fuller
- dyer
- webster
- tailor
- skinner
- soutar
- saddler
- miller
- baxter
- flesher
- blacksmith

5. Make two lists of the dangers and benefits of overseas trade.

Extension task

1. Carry out some research into the types of goods which may have been bought and sold in a market in the Middle Ages. Use the school resource centre, the Internet or a local library to find the information. Design a poster to present your findings.

10 The Wars of Independence – Phase 1 (1296–1305)

For years, the Scottish kings had been trying to win back land from the Vikings. In 1263, King Haakon IV of Norway led a large invasion fleet to the west coast of Scotland. What actually happened off the Ayrshire coast near Largs is still a matter of debate. Some or all of the Viking fleet was wrecked in a storm, and the army was driven ashore, where it was defeated by the Scots. Two months later, King Haakon died in Orkney.

— King Alexander III and the 'Golden Age'

Alexander III ruled Scotland during the thirteenth century. He began his reign aged eight in 1249, and became a very strong king.

Following the death of King Haakon, the new Norwegian king, Magnus, opened peace talks with Alexander and the Scots to try and put an end to invasions. In 1266, the Treaty of Perth was signed. The islands of the Hebrides (or Sudreys as the Norwegians called them) were granted to the Scots for a lump sum of money, while the Northern Isles – Orkney and Shetland – remained part of Norway. Scotland's northern and western borders were now clearly fixed, and this led the way to lasting peace between Scotland and Norway.

Throughout his reign, Alexander controlled the powerful nobles and tried to deal fairly with all his subjects. In the countryside, the peasants could grow their crops and rear their animals without fear of having them destroyed or stolen by invaders. Trade grew, and the towns or burghs prospered. By modern standards, Scotland was a very poor country, but life was improving for most people.

Family tree of the Scottish royal family. The dates show the years in reign as Scotland's king or queen. ▶

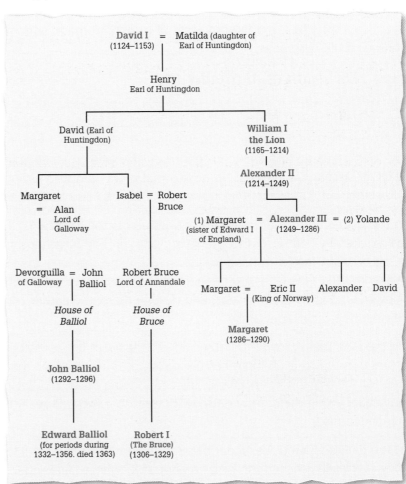

No heir to the throne?

Like his father Alexander II, Alexander III married an English princess, Margaret. She was the sister of the English king, King Edward I, and this marriage helped to keep the peace with England. In 1281, Alexander III's daughter, Margaret, married King Eric of Norway. This marriage also helped to maintain good relations between Scotland and its neighbours and put off the threat of attack.

This period of peace from 1266–81 is known as the 'Golden Age', but unfortunately it did not last. Alexander's wife died in 1275, but England and Scotland remained allies. Tragically, all three of Alexander's children died before him, including Prince Alexander, the heir to the throne. Despite these blows, Alexander continued to rule fairly. He and his barons agreed in 1285 that his grand-daughter and only surviving close relative, Princess Margaret – also known as 'the Maid of Norway' (as she lived in Norway) – would become the heir to the throne.

However, this arrangement had its problems. Princess Margaret was only one year old, far too young to rule Scotland if anything happened to Alexander. Also, it was unusual for females to rule European countries during the Middle Ages.

Later in 1285, there was great rejoicing when Alexander re-married. His new wife was Yolande, daughter of a Norman baron. It was hoped that they would produce a male heir and the problems of having Margaret as the heir to the throne would disappear.

40

The death of Alexander III

On 18 March 1286 in the Great Hall of Edinburgh Castle, Alexander was having a meeting of his Grand Council, made up of the chief barons of Scotland. Outside, a violent storm was raging. When the meeting was over, the king prepared to travel to Kinghorn in Fife, where Queen Yolande was staying. Despite the pleas of his nobles that it was too wild a night to travel, Alexander left Edinburgh, making for the Queen's Ferry at Dalmeny.

In the Middle Ages there were no bridges across the Firth of Forth. Travellers were taken by boat across to Fife. Even today, in bad weather there are often restrictions on the Forth Road Bridge. At Dalmeny, the ferry-man warned Alexander that it was far too dangerous to cross the two miles of stormy sea. Alexander ignored his warnings, and despite the bad weather conditions, they reached the other side safely.

By the time they reached the other side of the Forth it was dark and the storm was raging even more fiercely. Alexander turned down the offer of a bed for the night in Inverkeithing. Instead, he and his guides set off on horseback along the narrow path by the seashore. No one really knows what happened next.

In the darkness, King Alexander became separated from his guides. When they eventually reached the king's manor at Kinghorn, Alexander was no

The last journey of King Alexander from Edinburgh to Kinghorn. ▼

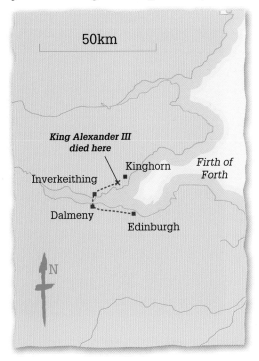

50km

King Alexander III died here

Inverkeithing
Kinghorn
Firth of Forth
Dalmeny
Edinburgh

N

longer with them. The next morning, the king was found lying at the bottom of a cliff with a broken neck. In the darkness, his horse probably stumbled and fell, throwing Alexander to his death. The spot is now marked by a memorial.

All Scotland mourned. The country was without a king. Following the 1285 agreement, Margaret would now be queen, but she was only three years old. Scotland was in trouble as there was no suitable leader.

Source A

When Alexander our king was dead,
That Scotland ruled in love and lee
Away was wealth of ale and bread,
Of wine and wax, of game and glee
Our gold was changed into lead.
Then cry to God, for only He
Can save us in perplexity.

The feelings of many Scots upon the death of Alexander III (by an unknown writer of the time).

41

Questions

1. Explain how royal marriages helped to keep the peace in the Middle Ages.

2. **a.** What important agreement did Alexander make with his barons in 1285?
   b. Why might this agreement cause problems? (Try to think of two reasons.)

3. Why do you think Alexander decided to make his journey, even though the weather was so bad?

4. Read the poem in Source A carefully. What do you think the writer means when he says 'our gold was changed into lead'?

Extension task

1. Take a full page in your workbook. Alternatively, your teacher may provide you with a piece of A4 paper. Design the front page of a newspaper, telling of King Alexander's death. This should include:

   ● An appropriate headline
   ● An article about the king's tragic accident, including a map of his last journey
   ● An article about what might happen now that the king is dead
   ● At least one suitable illustration.

Margaret and the succession problem

The new queen, Margaret, was just three years old when she inherited the throne. As she was so young, six guardians were appointed to rule Scotland on her behalf, until she was old enough to rule on her own. The six men included two bishops of the Church and four nobles. It was hoped that these guardians would keep the country united and stop any powerful nobleman from trying to claim the throne by force. One such man, Robert Bruce, Lord of Annandale, did try to take control of Scotland. Although his rebellion was easily put down, it showed how dangerous the situation was.

King Edward I of England. ▶

Another threat to Scotland's stability came from outside Scotland. King Edward I of England (the great uncle of Margaret) wanted to unite the two countries under his control. Edward was also worried that trouble or rebellions in Scotland could spill over into England. Soon, discussions began between the Scots, the King of Norway and King Edward. It was agreed that Margaret should leave Norway (her home) and come to Scotland to take up the throne by 1290. Edward also proposed that his son, Prince Edward, should marry Margaret. The guardians agreed to this in return for a guarantee that Scotland would remain independent from England. This was officially agreed in the Treaty of Birgham, signed in July 1290.

Margaret was still only seven years old when she set out from the port of Bergen in Norway. Then tragedy struck; she was taken ill during the long sea voyage. Soon after reaching Orkney, she died. Everyone was shocked by the news. Scotland now had a crisis over the succession to the throne. Who would rule Scotland now?

Edward I was also stunned by the news. His plans to bring about a union of England and Scotland through a marriage alliance between Margaret and his son Edward were in ruins. There was not one surviving direct relative of the Scottish royal family. Soon after Margaret's death, Bishop Fraser of St Andrews, one of the six guardians, wrote to Edward asking for help (see Source C).

The decision to ask Edward to help the Scots was understandable.

- He was a neighbour.
- He was the late King Alexander's brother-in-law.
- He had great knowledge of the law.

There is fear of a general war and a great slaughter of men. Let your excellency come with troops towards the border, to help save the shedding of blood, and choose for king him who of right ought to have the succession.

A letter from Bishop Fraser of St Andrews to Edward I, 1290.

At this time Edward was 51 years of age. He had recently conquered Wales, and already ruled Ireland and large parts of France. There were many in England who thought that Edward should now take his chance to control Scotland, too. Edward agreed to judge the claims of all those who said they should be King of Scotland.

There were thirteen nobles who put themselves forward – they were called competitors. Edward marched to the Scottish border with an army. He insisted that the Scots should accept him as their overlord (feudal superior). The Scots were not keen on this, but eventually agreed. Edward listened to all the claims for the throne. By August 1292, only two nobles remained whose claims he had not rejected, Robert Bruce, Lord of Annandale and John Balliol, Lord of Galloway.

Questions

1. Why was the death of Margaret, the Maid of Norway, such a tragedy?

2. Why did the Scots ask King Edward to help them to choose a king?

3. Look carefully at Source C. Why does Bishop Fraser ask King Edward to come to the border?

4. Study the family tree on page 39 and answer these questions:

   a. Who was the grandson of William I?
   b. What relation were William I and David, Earl of Huntingdon?
   c. Who was the elder daughter of David, Earl of Huntingdon?
   d. Who was the son of Isabel?
   e. Weighing up all the evidence, write down the name of the rightful King of Scotland.

Extension tasks

1. In groups of three or four, design a series of three or four posters for a wall display to show the main events in Scotland beween the death of Alexander III and the choice of John Balliol as king. Use a mixture of writing and visuals.

2. Write down why your group chose these scenes and events, and be prepared to justify these decisions to the rest of the class in a class discussion.

John Balliol and Edward's invasion

John Balliol was crowned king at Scone on St Andrew's Day, 1292 as he was the rightful King of Scotland according to the rules of succession. Very quickly, John discovered that Edward did not intend to leave him alone to rule Scotland. Soon, the English king was interfering in Scottish affairs.

Source D

John Balliol (kneeling) paying homage to Edward I. ▶

43

John always did as Edward asked. The Scottish barons were dismayed by John's apparent weakness, and urged him to stand up to Edward. England went to war against France in 1294 and Edward expected that the Scots would help him by sending an army. Some barons did, but others pressed John to disobey Edward. He refused, so the Scottish barons took control of the country. Twelve guardians were appointed to rule Scotland. In John's name, these guardians made a treaty with the French king, Philip IV, to fight against the English (instead of *with* the English). To Edward this was **treason**, a crime against the monarch, and such behaviour had to be punished.

An English army marched over the border in 1294 and besieged Berwick, Scotland's richest town. Hundreds of men, women and children were killed and the town was destroyed. At Dunbar, Edward defeated the Scottish army, which was smaller and less well-equipped than the English. Edinburgh Castle surrendered after a three-day siege, and Stirling Castle was also taken. The two most important royal fortresses were now in English hands.

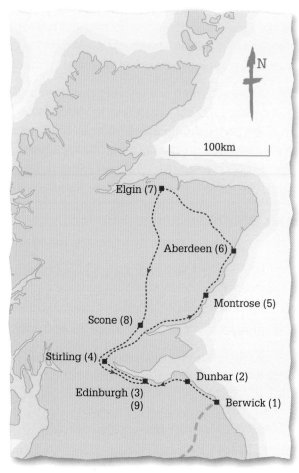

The route of Edward's invasion.

Further resistance to Edward seemed useless. At Montrose, John's symbols of kingship – his family insignia and tabard (jacket) – were ripped from him, a ceremony designed to show that he was not even worthy to be a knight, never mind a king. Because of this, John became known as 'Toom Tabard' (the man with the empty coat). He was sent to prison in England on charges of treason.

Edward continued his march northwards, capturing the towns of Aberdeen and Elgin. Then he turned and made his way south again. Before he left Scotland, Edward removed important documents and symbols of Scotland's independence. These included the Stone of Destiny from Scone and the crown and sceptre from Edinburgh Castle. By the end of August 1296, over 1500 leading barons, bishops and burgesses had been forced to swear an oath of allegiance to Edward. They put their seal on pieces of parchment which were sown together and known as the 'Ragman's Roll'. Edward then arranged for Scotland to be ruled in his name.

Questions

1. Why did John Balliol prove to be a weak king?

2. Describe what happened after Edward went to war with France in 1294.

3. Using the map of Scotland, write down what happened in each of the places marked 1 to 9 on the map.

44

William Wallace: Man of mystery

Following Edward's invasion of Scotland in 1294, the English now had strongholds in all parts of the countryside and in the castles of Scotland. Edward appointed the Earl of Surrey as Governor of Scotland and Hugh Cressingham as Treasurer (in charge of finances). Other Englishmen were appointed as sheriffs, to rule counties or shires like Lanark or Stirling and to keep law and order. Their rule was harsh and this made them unpopular with the Scottish people. Soon rebellions began. The first was a revolt of nobles in the south-west. Others, more serious, broke out under the leadership of Andrew Murray in the north and William Wallace (Sources E and F).

Linking up with Andrew Murray, in August 1297, Wallace moved from Dundee towards Stirling. Although most of the rebellious Scots nobles had surrendered to the English the previous month, more and more of Scotland was slipping out of English control. Surrey and Cressingham gathered a large army and marched north to crush the rebellious Scots.

Source E

There was a public robber called William Wallace, who had been outlawed many times because he would not accept Edward as king. Because he was a wandering outlaw, he attracted all the other bandits to himself and made himself almost their prince. They grew to be a large group.

Walter of Guisborough, an Englishman writing in 1297.

Source F

In 1297, William Wallace murdered the English Sheriff of Lanark. From that time all those people who hated the English flocked to him and he became their leader. He was wondrously brave and bold, but some of the lords of the kingdom looked down on him because he was low born.

John of Fordun, a Scotsman writing in the fourteenth century.

45

The Battle of Stirling Bridge

Wallace's greatest triumph was the defeat of the English army at Stirling Bridge on 11 September 1297.

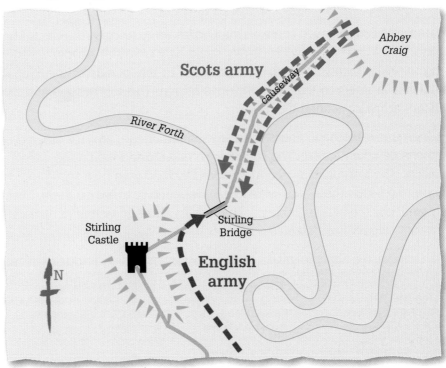

A plan of the Battle of Stirling Bridge. ▶

Source G

The Battle of Stirling Bridge,
a nineteenth-century painting
by Sir William Hole. ▲

Source H

A statue of William Wallace in Aberdeen. ▲

Wallace and his small, inexperienced army were on the north side of the bridge, and the large, experienced English army was advancing from the south. Wallace allowed some of the English army to cross the bridge before attacking them. The English cavalry could only cross the narrow wooden bridge two abreast. Once they had crossed to the far side of the river, it was difficult for them to move quickly or to retreat. The soft ground and their heavy armour weighed them down.

When a few thousand English had crossed the bridge, Wallace ordered his men to charge down the hill. The English who had crossed the bridge were cut to pieces. The rest found the bridge blocked by their own men trying to run away from the Scots. Thousands were killed, wounded or drowned in the river, and then finally the bridge collapsed. This was an amazing victory; an amateur army of foot soldiers had defeated a superior, more experienced enemy.

In October the Scots followed up their victory at Stirling Bridge by recapturing most of the English-held castles. Berwick was recaptured, and the north of England was raided. In March 1298, Wallace was knighted and appointed Guardian of Scotland in the name of King John. Wallace gained the support of the Church by appointing William Lamberton, a loyal supporter of Scottish independence, as Bishop of St Andrews.

Group decision-making assignment

Work in groups of three or four for this. Use the information below to help you. Your group has to advise William Wallace about what he should do.

Imagine you are with Wallace and his army on the north side of the River Forth. Your army is small and has never fought a large battle. You have very few knights. A messenger arrives to say that a large English army is coming towards you from the other side of the river. There are many knights in this army and they have fought many battles. There is only one narrow wooden bridge across the River Forth between you and the English army.

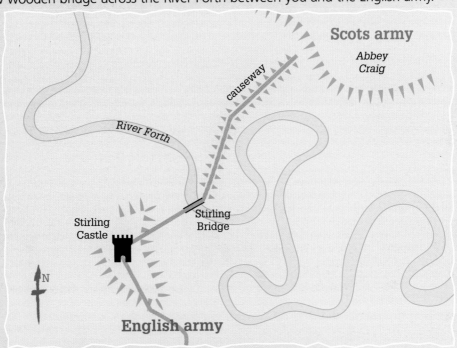

Sketch map of the Battle of Stirling Bridge area.

These are the options available to William Wallace:

a. Run away.

b. Go across the bridge to meet the English army in the open.

c. Let some of the English army come across the bridge before attacking them.

d. Let the entire English army come across the bridge and meet them in the open.

1. Which of the options would you advise and why?

――― *From victory to defeat: the Battle of Falkirk*

Meanwhile, King Edward was planning massive retaliation for the English defeat. Returning from France, where he had been fighting, Edward amassed a huge army of 2000 knights and 12,000 foot-soldiers, including archers and crossbowmen. Retreating before this vast army, Wallace and his men took up a defensive position east of Falkirk.

47

Extension task

Below is a list of facts about the situation before the Battle of Falkirk. In groups or pairs, discuss and decide which of them are advantages for the Scottish army and which are disadvantages. Copy the table into your workbooks and write down the points in the correct column.

- The Scottish army was up on a hillside.
- The Scottish army was smaller than the English army.
- In front of the Scottish army was a small loch (lake).
- Behind the Scottish army was rough woodland.
- The Scots had about 500 knights.
- The Scots had a few archers.
- The Scottish army was behind a barrier of wooden stakes.

Advantages for the Scots	Disadvantages for the Scots

Wallace had organised the Scottish foot-soldiers into four circular formations called **schiltrons**. With one row of spearmen kneeling and one row standing and the spears of the schiltron pointing outwards, the cavalry would find the circles difficult to penetrate. The few Scots archers were placed between the schiltrons.

The Battle of Falkirk was not to be a repeat of the Scottish victory at Stirling Bridge. The power of the English cavalry charge made the Scots knights and archers scatter. The English archers, with their longbows and crossbows were able to create gaps in the schiltrons. The English knights on horseback were then able to charge through these gaps. Wallace had no option but to retreat from the battlefield. Thousand of Scots were killed.

Scots knights
Archers
Scottish schiltrons
Barrier of wooden stakes
Loch/river
English knights
Edward's army
English archers

▲ *A plan of the Battle of Falkirk.*

William Wallace took full responsibility for the defeat. He resigned as Guardian of Scotland, and for the next seven years very little is known about his movements. Edward, satisfied that his victory had ended Scottish resistance for good, returned to the war in France.

48

The capture and execution of William Wallace

Following his defeat at Falkirk, Wallace travelled to Europe to try to raise support for Scotland's independence and to free John Balliol from prison. He visited Rome and persuaded Pope Boniface to condemn Edward's occupation of Scotland. As a result of the Pope's intervention, John Balliol was released.

At the same time, the Scots continued the struggle against English rule. Two barons, John Comyn and Robert Bruce, Earl of Carrick, had replaced Wallace as joint guardians. This was not a very successful arrangement, as the two men hated each other so did not co-operate very well. In 1300 Bruce resigned and later surrendered to Edward in order to keep his lands. By 1304, most Scottish barons had submitted to Edward. Stirling Castle was finally given up to the English in July 1304 after a three-month siege.

Wallace, however, refused to surrender, even though he was declared an outlaw by the Scottish authorities. We know from written evidence that he remained active in resisting the English, but historians have little or no evidence about his movements. Eventually, with the surrender of most Scottish nobles and resistance at a low level, Wallace was captured near Glasgow on 3 August 1305 by a Scottish knight, Sir John Menteith, who handed him over to the English. He was taken to London to be tried at Westminster Hall. He was accused of treason and other crimes, and as an outlaw was not allowed to defend himself. Wallace was found guilty and sentenced to death (Source I).

Source I

It is resolved that William Wallace be tied to a hurdle and dragged from the Palace of Westminster to the Tower of London, and then through the middle of the city as far as Smithfield, where he is to be hanged. Afterwards, his head is to be cut off and fixed above London Bridge for all to see. His heart, kidneys, lungs and other internal organs are to be burned. Then his body is to be cut into four quarters. One is to be hanged on a gibbet at Newcastle, one at Berwick, the third at Stirling and the fourth at Perth, as a warning to those who pass by and see them.

Verdict of Edward's judges on William Wallace.

49

Questions

1. Describe Wallace's actions after losing the Battle of Falkirk.

2. Explain what happened in Scotland after the Battle of Falkirk. Did resistance continue and was it successful?

3. Read Source I.
   a. Why do you think Wallace was to be dragged through the streets of London before his execution?
   b. Explain why Wallace was executed in this way.

Extended writing

1. Using all the information from this section, write an obituary to illustrate the life and career of William Wallace. Use the following headings to help you.
   - Early life
   - Battle successes
   - Battle defeats
   - Later life

11 The Wars of Independence – Phase 2 (1306–57)

King Edward was now certain that the death of Wallace had ended Scottish resistance to English rule. However, in 1306, less than a year after Wallace's death, a new leader appeared to challenge Edward – Robert Bruce.

—— Robert Bruce and the murder at Greyfriars

Robert Bruce, Earl of Carrick and Lord of Annandale, was the grandson of one of the competitors for the throne of Scotland in 1292. He was a powerful baron with estates in France, England and the south of Scotland. Although he had supported Edward since 1301, he was an ambitious man. He realised that if the Scots could be led by a strong king, they could defeat the English and drive them out of Scotland.

Source A

A nineteenth-century painting of Robert Bruce (second from left) and others, by Sir William Hole. This is a detail from a much larger painting. ▲

Bruce had a rival to the throne – John Comyn (who also had a claim to the Scottish throne as he was the nephew of John Balliol). A meeting between the two men was arranged at Greyfriars church in Dumfries on 10 February 1306. At some time during the meeting, the two quarrelled and Bruce struck Comyn with a dagger, wounding him. The meeting ended with more violence, as Bruce's supporters killed Comyn and his uncle. This was a shocking event. Many people turned against Bruce after the murder at Greyfriars. Bruce was excommunicated – completely cut off from the Church – and declared an outlaw.

King in name only

With the threat from Comyn and his supporters removed temporarily, Bruce and his followers captured several castles in south-west Scotland. Bruce then travelled to Scone, the centre of Scottish kingship. On 25 March 1306, he had himself proclaimed King of Scots in the presence of his four brothers, three bishops and several barons. Two days later he was crowned in a simple ceremony (Source B). There was no Stone of Destiny and no crown jewels. A simple circlet of gold was placed on Bruce's head by Isabel, Countess of Buchan, sister of the Earl of Fife. So began the reign of King Robert I.

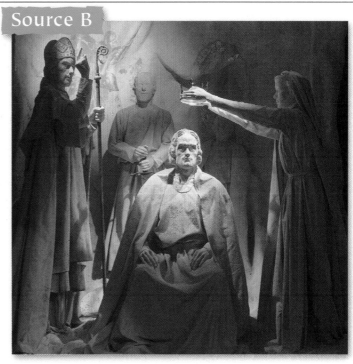

A stone sculpture showing Robert Bruce's coronation at Scone.

Source C

All those who were present at the death of Sir John Comyn are to be drawn and hanged. And all those who agreed to it, and those who afterwards received them willingly, knowing the deed was done, to have the same judgement. And those who are or will be captured bearing arms against the king be hanged or beheaded.

Edward's orders upon hearing of the events in Scotland.

Edward I, on hearing the news of Bruce's coronation was eager to get rid of this new king who rebelled against his own rule. Bruce and his small army were scattered by an English force under Sir Aymer de Valence at Methven, near Perth on 19 June 1306. Edward confiscated Bruce's estates, executed three of his brothers and imprisoned his wife and sister. Bruce left mainland Scotland at this point, his cause seemingly hopeless.

51

Questions

1. Why did the events in Dumfries on 10 February 1306 cause Bruce to lose support?

2. In what ways was Bruce's coronation different from that of other Scottish kings?

3. Why was Bruce 'king in name only'?

Extension task

1. Find out as much as you can about the legend of Bruce and the spider using your school resource centre and the Internet.

The return of Robert Bruce

In the spring of 1307, Bruce decided to return to Scotland, landing near some of his confiscated lands in Ayrshire. He decided to engage in **guerrilla warfare** against his enemies, who were much more numerous.

Within seven years of returning to the Scottish mainland, Robert Bruce became master of all Scotland (in 1314). How was this possible after such a disastrous start, when even most Scots were against him? He had powerful enemies among the Scottish barons, many of whom still supported the cause of King John Balliol.

There are several important factors which contributed to Bruce's success.

- Bruce was a very skilful and ruthless military commander.
- King Edward I died in July 1307.
- Bruce was a clever and astute political leader as well as a good soldier.

Secret warfare

Bruce's English opponents called his tactics against them 'secret warfare'. Bruce knew that his forces would be destroyed in open battle, so he used what is now called guerrilla warfare. He won two small victories against much larger English forces, at Glentrool in Galloway in April 1307, and at Loudon Hill in Ayrshire in May of the same year. Edward I again set out to invade Scotland to punish Bruce and put an end to his rebellions. By this time Edward was 68 and was seriously ill, but he was carried on a litter at the head of his army.

52

Edward I, carried on a litter on his last march into Scotland.

Edward died at Burgh-on-Sands near Carlisle in 1307, within sight of the Scottish border. His son, Edward II, was not interested in fighting and called off the invasion, returning south to bury his father. On his tomb at Westminster Abbey is inscribed in Latin:

HIC IACET EDWARDUS PRIMUS, MALLEUS SCOTTORUM
(Here lies Edward First, Hammer of the Scots)

Scottish enemies

For the next two years, Bruce and his supporters fought a civil war. His main Scottish enemies, the Comyns and the MacDougalls, were each defeated in turn. After victory over the Comyns near Inverurie in Aberdeenshire, Bruce's men destroyed the Comyn lands and livestock in the 'Herschip of Buchan' (an act of looting and revenge).

Source E

His men through Buchan did he send
To burn and slay from end to end
He ravaged it in such a way
That fifty years beyond that day
The rape of Buchan was still grieved.

Verse by a medieval poet.

By the summer of 1308, all the barons in the north-east of Scotland had submitted to Bruce and all but one of the castles were in his hands. The MacDougalls in the west were ambushed and slaughtered at the Pass of Brander beside Loch Awe in Argyll, caught between Bruce's forces and Highlanders led by Sir James Douglas.

Capturing the castles

More and more barons were now coming on to Bruce's side. A parliament in St Andrews in 1309 declared him the rightful king, and Church leaders supported him, despite the murder at Greyfriars. By 1312, most of Scotland had been regained. However, some of the main castles remained in English hands. The Scots had no money to buy expensive siege equipment. Instead they captured castles by clever tactics which took the defenders by surprise.

Source F

The capture of Linlithgow Castle.

53

Linlithgow Castle in West Lothian was captured when some Scots hid in a cart-load of hay being sent to the castle by a local farmer. Once at the gatehouse, the cart stopped. The Scots jumped out and were joined by others who had hidden themselves outside the castle. The English were quickly overwhelmed. Like all the other castles, Linlithgow was demolished, so that it would be of no use to the English if recaptured.

By the summer of 1313, only one castle remained in English hands – Stirling. Robert Bruce's brother, Edward Bruce, besieged it for many months, but the English were able to hold out because they received supplies by ship along the River Forth. Eventually, Edward Bruce made an agreement with the castle governor, Sir Philip Moubray which said that if an English army did not come to relieve the defenders of Stirling Castle by midsummer 1314, the castle would be surrendered to the Scots. From that date all the castles of Scotland would then be free from English rule. Edward II responded by gathering a huge army to defend Stirling Castle. This led to the most decisive event in the struggle for independence from England; the Battle of Bannockburn, 1314.

Questions

1. Why was the death of Edward I of benefit to Bruce's cause?

2. What was 'secret warfare' and why was it necessary?

3. Look at Source E and the text. What evidence is there that Bruce could be a cruel and ruthless leader?

4. How had Bruce gained more support by 1309?

5. Why were the Scots reluctant to lay siege to castles?

6. Explain how the Scots captured Linlithgow Castle.

7. What agreement was reached about Stirling Castle?

Extended writing

1. Find out more about how the Scots captured castles. You should be able to find information about Perth, Roxburgh and Edinburgh. Write a report entitled: Capturing the castles.

The Battle of Bannockburn, 1314

The English army

Edward ordered his army to gather at Wark near Berwick on 10 June 1314. His army was well-armed, well-trained and about 20,000 strong, thus outnumbering the Scots by three to one. There were three types of fighting men. The cavalry numbered about 2000, and comprised some of the bravest knights in Europe. The horsemen wore suits of chain-mail, covered by a surcoat on which their insignia was emblazoned – this showed which side they were fighting for. Each would have charged into battle with a four-metre long lance and carried a mace or battle axe for close combat. The horses wore trappers, coloured blankets which protected them against enemy spears.

The archers used longbows, each with a quiver of 24 metal-tipped arrows. Some of the best archers were Welsh. Their job was to scatter the enemy archers and then concentrate their fire on the spearmen, before the cavalry charged. The rest of the foot-soldiers were spearmen, who each carried a four-metre long spear, a shield and a sword or dagger. They wore quilted jackets and steel bacinets (helmets). There were also a number of Scots fighting for Edward II, mainly sworn enemies of Bruce like the Comyns and MacDougalls. Edward expected this strong body of men to bring him victory by a mass charge against the Scots foot soldiers.

The Scottish army

Bruce knew that to fight a pitched battle against superior forces required careful preparation if it was not to end in defeat, as Wallace had demonstrated at Falkirk.

The Scots were organised into four divisions of foot-soldiers and one of horsemen. The horsemen were light cavalry, commanded by Sir Robert Keith, whose job was to protect the foot-soldiers from the English archers. Each division was divided into three or four schiltrons of spearmen. Each spearman also carried a shield and a sword, axe or dagger and wore a bacinet similar to that of the English foot-soldier. The small number of Scottish archers came from Ettrick Forest in the Borders. In reserve were approximately 2000 'small folk' – farmers and townspeople.

Source G

A Scottish shield and claymore with the lion rampant flag. ▶

Although these 'small folk' lacked equipment and training, they were desperate to join in the fight.

The four divisions were commanded by Sir Thomas Randolph, the Earl of Moray, Sir Edward Bruce, Sir James Douglas and the king himself. All areas of Scotland were represented in the army, from clansmen from the Highlands to Border dalesmen. Although inferior in numbers, the Scots knew the ground well and the men and commanders had worked closely together for many years.

The battlefield

There is still a lot of debate about where exactly the battlefield was. Whatever the exact location, Bruce took time to prepare a strong defensive position south of Stirling. The Scots could look out to the east towards the River Forth over low ground called the Carse. On their right was thick forest. The English would have to approach from the south, on the old Roman road from Falkirk to Stirling. Bruce positioned his army on either side of the road, behind the Bannock Burn, where it ran through a deep gorge. Bruce further strengthened this position by digging rows of camouflaged pits and laying **calthrops** (sharp metal spikes) to lame the horses.

This position would force Edward either to attack head-on over ground that was too soft for the cavalry or risk going round the Scots' left flank through the Carse. On 22 June 1314, a report was brought to Bruce by his patrols that the English army was approaching. In spite of having marched more than 30 kilometres that day in the hot summer sun, they appeared to be in good shape.

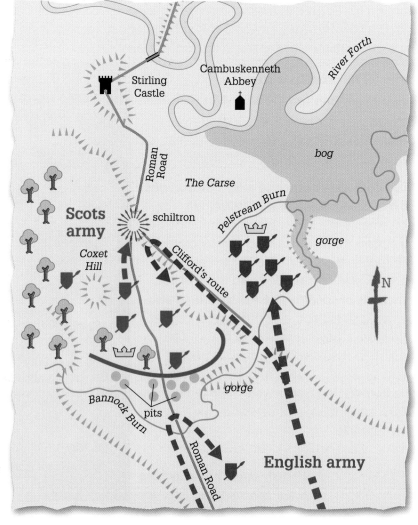

A plan of the Battle of Bannockburn. ▶

Questions

1. Copy the table below into your workbook. List the strengths and weaknesses of the two sides before the Battle of Bannockburn.

Strengths	Scots	English
1		
2		
3		
4		
Weaknesses		
1		
2		
3		
4		

2. Look carefully at the table you have completed. Which side do you think has the better chance to win the battle? Give your reasons.

The Battle of Bannockburn day one: Sunday 23 June

On 23 June, Edward's army set out from Falkirk. They had two days to relieve Stirling Castle, and were confident of victory. In the afternoon, Edward ordered a force of about 500 cavalry under Sir Robert Clifford to cross the Bannock Burn and make a dash along the edge of the Carse towards Stirling Castle. However, Randolph led his division down to cut them off. Forming a schiltron, they stopped the English charge in its tracks, and eventually drove them off.

Meanwhile, the main English force approached the Scots defences. An English knight, Sir Henry de Bohun, spotted Bruce at the front of his troops. He was not yet dressed for battle, and was mounted on a pony, not his charger. De Bohun recognised Bruce by his gold coronet and charged straight at him with his lance. Avoiding the lance, Bruce brought down the full weight of his battle axe on to de Bohun's head, killing him with a single blow. The king is said to have remarked, 'Alas, I have broken my good battle-axe'.

By the evening of Sunday, the English army had crossed the Bannock Burn, resting between there and the Pelstream, another tributary of the Forth. The Scots now realised that their enemies were in a very confined space, and thereby vulnerable to attack. Bruce was told of the low morale of the English, and, despite having far fewer soldiers, he decided to attack early the next morning – midsummer's day.

The Battle of Bannockburn day two: Monday 24 June

The Scots advanced at dawn on midsummer's day. The English were amazed to see them risking a battle in the open against superior forces.

The Earl of Gloucester led the cavalry against Edward Bruce's division, which immediately formed a schiltron and threw them back, killing Gloucester.

Douglas and Randolph moved their divisions forward to deal with the rest of the English army, which found it very difficult to get into formation properly because they were so hemmed in between the two streams. The Scots pushed forward slowly, but some English archers, breaking free from the crowd, started to shower arrows on the Scots. Seeing the danger, Bruce immediately sent Keith's light cavalry to deal with them. The archers were driven from the field.

Bruce ordered his own division into battle, and the English began to give ground, becoming a confused mass, as those at the back could not get into action. Edward II was persuaded to retreat to Stirling Castle, and this caused the English to waver. Finally, the 'small folk', kept hidden behind Coxet Hill, came charging down towards the English. Thinking they were fresh reserves rather than untrained and poorly armed volunteers, the English army disintegrated and fled in all directions. Some drowned in the river Forth, others in the Bannock Burn. King Edward was refused entry to Stirling Castle, so turned and fled to Dunbar, where he escaped by boat to Berwick.

Source H

58

▲ *A painting of the Battle of Bannockburn.*

Bruce's victory was now complete. All the English supplies were captured and many knights were held for ransom. It was said that Scotland became rich in a day, and it gained perhaps as much as £200,000 (worth more than £50 million in today's money). Bannockburn was more than just a victory. Stirling Castle was handed over so that Bruce was now in total control of his kingdom. Scotland was completely free and independent for the first time since the days of Alexander III. King Robert had proved himself to be a first-class military leader.

Questions

1. Imagine you were at Bannock Burn. Describe your experiences, making sure you mention the main events of the two-day battle.

   - Randolph v Clifford's knights.
   - The incident between Bruce and Sir Henry de Bohun.
   - The Scots attack at dawn on 24 June.
   - How the English archers were dealt with.
   - The part played by the 'small folk'.
   - The final victory.

2. Why did the Scots win against all the odds? Use all the evidence to help you to give as many reasons as possible.

Extension task

1. In groups of three or four, produce a poster illustrating the story of Bannock Burn. Your poster should include some of the following information, but you may vary it to suit your own ideas.

   - A heading with a victory/freedom slogan.
   - A picture of a triumphant Robert Bruce.
   - Written information about the two armies.
   - Weapons and armour used at the battle.
   - The main events of the battle in words and pictures.
   - A plan or diagram of the battlefield.

59

Free at last?

Despite the victory of the Scots, the war was not over. Edward II refused to recognise Scotland's independence. He still claimed to be overlord of Scotland. For fourteen years, Bruce played a waiting game. The north of England was raided several times, but Edward II remained stubborn. He also had the support of the new Pope, who excommunicated Bruce and four Scottish bishops. It was important for the Scots to convince the Pope that his support for Edward was wrong.

The Declaration of Arbroath

In 1320, about 50 of the most powerful barons sent a letter to the Pope. This now famous document was the Declaration of Arbroath. The letter was designed to show that Scotland had always been independent, that Edward I had been a cruel oppressor, and that Robert Bruce was the rightful king. It helped to persuade the Pope to recognise Bruce as king and end his excommunication. Its most famous passage is shown in Source I.

Source I

For so long as a hundred of us remain alive, we shall never agree to bow down to English rule. It is not for glory, nor honours nor riches that we fight, but for freedom alone, which no worthy man loses except with his life.

Extract from the Declaration of Arbroath, 1320.

Source J

◀ *The great seal of Robert Bruce on the charter granted to Melrose in 1326.*

The Treaty of Edinburgh, 1328

In 1327, Edward II was deposed and murdered. His successor, Edward III agreed to peace talks with the Scots, which took place in Edinburgh in March 1328. The terms were **ratified** (agreed to) by the English Parliament at Northampton soon afterwards. The treaty stated that the English king would give up all claims over Scotland and recognise Robert Bruce as king of a free nation, independent of English rule.

By the time the Treaty of Edinburgh was signed, Robert Bruce was very ill and he died at Cardross on the River Clyde on 7 June 1329, aged 55. He was buried at Dunfermline Abbey. His dying wish was for his heart to be taken to the Holy Land. His faithful friend, Sir James Douglas, set out with a band of knights to fulfil his wish, but was killed by the Moors in Spain. Douglas' body and Bruce's heart were recovered and returned to Scotland. Bruce's heart was buried at Melrose Abbey.

The Treaty of Edinburgh did not bring lasting peace between Scotland and England. The new king, David II, was only five years old when his father Robert Bruce died. Many barons who had lost their lands during the Wars of Independence – the so-called **Disinherited** – saw a chance to win their lands back. In 1332, Edward Balliol, son of the disgraced King John, invaded Scotland and defeated David's forces at Dupplin Moor near Perth. Six weeks later, Balliol was crowned King of Scots at Scone. Edward III (the English king) openly supported Balliol, crushing the Scots easily at the Battle of Halidon Hill near Berwick in July 1333. As Balliol continually received support from England, it was clear that Scotland had not really become independent. It would take many years before Scotland truly recovered independence. The fighting did not end until 1357, when the Treaty of Berwick was signed.

Questions

1. Why did the wars between Scotland and England not end with the Battle of Bannockburn?

2. Why was the Declaration of Arbroath written?

3. Look at Source I. What does it say is the main reason that the Scots were fighting?

5. What was Bruce's dying wish? Why? What happened?

6. Why did the wars start up again in 1332? When did they finally end?

12 Scotland at peace?

After the Treaty of Berwick ended the fighting, David II ruled until 1371. As he had no direct descendants, he was succeeded by his nephew Robert Stewart, who became Robert II. So began a long line of Scottish monarchs of this name, who ruled Scotland until 1603, when James VI of Scotland became James I of England in the Union of the Crowns. Today's British royal family is descended from the Stewart family.

Scotland's new dynasty

Historians disagree about the Stewart dynasty. The traditional view is that they were weak kings who often had to fight against powerful nobles. The fact that most of them became kings when too young to rule also caused problems. More recently, some historians have questioned this view, arguing that in the context of events in Europe at the time, the Stewarts did well. There were fewer rebellions against them than English kings experienced, and despite continued conflict on the disputed border between England and Scotland, the country managed to retain its independence.

Source A

Robert the second and first of ye race of ye stewarts. Began fi 1371

Robert II with his wife depicted in a sixteenth-century manuscript of Scottish kings and heraldry. ▶

⎯ *Two nations?*

As we have seen, large parts of the Highlands and Islands were ruled by the Vikings until the twelfth and thirteenth centuries. In these areas, real power was in the hands of local chiefs. Even when the Western Isles became Scottish in 1266, the chiefs were still important. The Highlands were far away from the centres of royal power in the Lowlands, and the way of life was different there. Most Highlanders spoke Gaelic, while Lowlanders spoke either English or French.

Source B

English is spoken by the people who live in the low country and on the coasts, and they are friendly, peaceful and wear decent clothes. Gaelic is spoken by the people who live in the Highlands and Islands. They are savage and untamed, wear ugly clothes, are liable to steal your goods and although kind to friends, are hostile and unmerciful to those who speak English.

A Lowlander (John of Fordun) writing in 1380.

The most important chief was the Lord of the Isles, who controlled a large area in the western Highlands. During the Wars of Independence, Robert Bruce defeated the MacDougall Lord of the Isles and replaced him by Angus Og, a MacDonald chief, who fought with Bruce at Bannockburn. By 1450, the MacDonalds controlled nearly all the Highlands. Scottish kings were usually engaged in other matters and did not control the area directly, so the Lord of the Isles was often treated like an independent king. In 1493, King James IV abolished the Lordship of the Isles. However, this did not solve all the problems. The differences between the Highlands and the Lowlands continued to cause difficulties until the eighteenth century.

⎯ *Scotland and Europe*

Robert Bruce signed a treaty with the French king in 1326, in which the two kings promised to support each other in any future war with England. This became known as the **Auld Alliance**, and continued for several centuries. The Auld Alliance was popular with most Scots because it meant that Scotland was treated as an equal, independent nation by the most powerful country in Europe. But it also led to Scotland becoming involved in sometimes unnecessary conflict with England.

Scotland had many other links with Europe, mainly through trade. Scottish wool from the borders was exported to the Low Countries (modern day Belgium and the Netherlands) where it was made into fine cloth in towns like Bruges and Ghent. Flemish and German merchants lived and worked in Berwick, and after 1400 many Scottish merchants could be found in cities

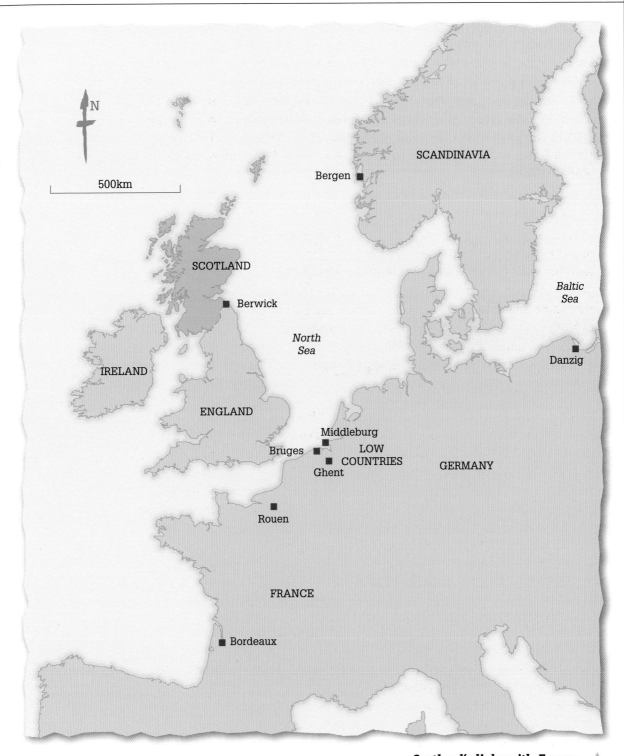

Scotland's links with Europe. ▲

such as Bruges, Danzig, Bergen, Bordeaux and Rouen. The most important place that Scots traded with was the Low Countries, where they had a staple port at Middleburg. This meant that the port had the right to control trade with Scotland. Many goods were taken back to Scotland from Middleburg in exchange for Scots wool and leather.

By 1450, Scotland was established as an independent kingdom with links to most of Europe. Even though the Stewart dynasty was eventually to lead Scotland into a union with England, the strong sense of Scottish nationhood forged during the Wars of Independence meant that this would be a union of equals and not conquest. The sense of Scottishness has continued up to the present day. The return of a Scottish parliament in 1999 is only the most recent reminder of this clear sense of identity.

Questions

1. Look at Source B. What evidence is there that John of Fordun was biased against the Highlanders?

2. What was the Auld Alliance and why was it important?

3. What was Scotland's main export in the Middle Ages?

4. Explain the meaning of a staple port. Where was Scotland's staple port?

Extension task

1. Look back to the timeline of the Middle Ages (page 4). Copy the timeline into your workbook and add all the key events and developments mentioned in this book.